Well, Doc, It Seemed Like A Good Idea At the Time!

The Unexpected Adventures of a Trauma Surgeon

Publisher and distributor:

Lighted Candle Society

P.O. Box 721

Bountiful, UT 84011

Attn: John L. Harmer, Esq.

Edited by Elayne Wells Harmer

Cover design by Darren Nelson

Interior layout and design by www.writingnights.org

Book preparation by Chad Robertson and Elayne Wells Harmer

ISBN: 978-171-9944595
LIBRARY OF CONGRESS CATALOGING-IN-PUBLICATION DATA:
NAMES: Waymack, J. Paul, M.D., Sc.D. author | Wells Harmer, Elayne, editor
TITLE: Well, Doc, It Seemed Like A Good Idea at the Time! –
The Unexpected Adventures of a Trauma Surgeon / J. Paul Waymack
DESCRIPTION: Independently Published, 2019.
IDENTIFIERS: ISBN 978-1-7199445-9-5 (Perfect bound) |
SUBJECTS: Surgeon | Hospital Residency | Memoir |
US Military | Medical Training --Popular works.
CLASSIFICATION: Pending

DEDICATION

This book is dedicated to all the nurses who kept me out of trouble—or at least tried to—during my surgical career. I give special thanks to Jane, Randi, and Andy, three of the finest nurses in the medical profession. It was truly a privilege to work with them.

I also dedicate this book to the unknown student who slipped into the computer science registration line at Virginia Tech just five seconds before me in July 1971, taking the last spot in a class I needed for my major. Had he arrived after me, I likely would have led a normal life as a chemical engineer and would have witnessed none of what I am about to relate. That student completely changed my life.

CONTENTS

Acknowledgments

I began recording the events in this book in the 1970s, when I was a third-year medical student. The journaling continued through my surgery residency, graduate school training, academic surgery career, and my service in the U.S. Army's Institute for Surgical Research; I finally stopped in the mid-1990s, when I worked at the FDA. By that time, the narratives were all stored in Word files on my hard drive, where they stayed, untouched, for 20 years.

One night several years ago, I had dinner with John Harmer, a friend and colleague. I mentioned offhand that I had kept a journal of memorable events, and John asked me to email him a copy. He had written and published half a dozen books throughout his distinguished political and legal career, and had a seasoned eye for a good narrative. After reading my 500 pages of journal entries, John insisted I turn the manuscript into a book. He asked if he could share it with an accomplished writer and editor, Elayne Wells Harmer, who happened to be his daughter-in-law. I agreed.

For the next six months, Elayne expertly condensed and edited many of my anecdotes and created this book. I will be eternally grateful for her efforts and John's encouragement. But for them, these stories would never have escaped my hard drive.

I would also like to thank all my professors, from my undergraduate years at Virginia Tech and medical school years at the Medical College of Virginia to my surgery residency and subsequent graduate school years at the University of Cincinnati. Their training enabled me to become a successful physician and surgeon and to experience what I am about to relate.

Finally, I would like to thank all my patients. Although it is true that at times some of them showed a total lack of judgment—hence the common refrain, "Well, Doc, it seemed like a good idea at the time"—most of them showed incredible courage in dealing with life's greatest struggles. Such courage was always a source of amazement and inspiration to me. I hope I can show half the courage they did when I am faced with such challenges.

J. Paul Waymack, M.D., Sc.D.
September 2017

Prologue

IN JULY 1976, I began my third year as a medical student at the Medical College of Virginia in Richmond, Virginia. After two cloistered years studying textbooks and cadavers in classrooms and labs, I was relieved and eager to finally move over to clinical rotations in a handful of Virginia hospitals.

My first rotation was in the emergency room of Riverside Hospital in Newport News, an hour east of the Medical College. As I drove to the hospital that first sunny morning, I was filled with excitement at the prospect of finally spending my days seeing patients—but more than a little nervous about the probability of making mistakes in front of them. Still, I was naively confident that I would be skilled, professional, and respected, and I thought I knew something about the types of cases doctors handled. I expected patients would present with fevers, chest pains, a broken leg, or maybe even a gunshot wound. I expected patients would look and act the way my family had always behaved when we visited the doctor's office.

In other words, I was utterly unprepared for the insanity I would encounter that day, or during the years that followed.

That morning, I didn't envision myself chasing naked patients around the ER parking lot in the middle of the night. I never imagined I'd use a horse sling to transfer a 700-pound patient. I certainly didn't expect to be treating a patient who, after running away from the hospital, leaped into a passing convertible and then swallowed the cigarette lighter. And I most definitely never guessed that one day I would be a major in the U.S. Army Medical Corps during the Cold War, on orders of the president and with a KGB agent hot on my tail, or that I would find a long-deceased corpse in the intensive care unit in a remote hospital in the Soviet Union.

In my wildest dreams I never imagined most of what I experienced as a doctor, but these stories are all true. I couldn't have made them up if I tried.

As I began to realize that my career as a trauma physician would not be at all what I had anticipated, I started keeping a record of the various insane events I witnessed. This book is a look back at some of the more memorable ones. Of course, I certainly witnessed my share of tragedies and discouragement, but it was the lighter side of human behavior that I chose to record. Much like the novel and television show *M*A*S*H*, based on a surgeon's memoirs of his service behind the front lines of the Korean War, this book tries to capture the humorous anecdotes in the life of a surgeon.

The experiences recounted here are authentic. In most instances, names of patients and doctors have been changed to protect their privacy.

Part I
The Student

1976-1978

The First Day

ON MY FIRST DAY as a brand-new third-year medical student on rotation in the emergency room at Riverside Hospital, I cheerfully introduced myself to the ER director, the intern, the nurses, the receptionist, and anybody else I passed. Although I was just a medical student, I had the self-assurance and buoyancy of a promising doctor, and I was eager to meet the staff and get to work.

The director showed me the doctors' lounge. It was located right in the middle of the ER, and doctors retreated there to read charts, write notes, review X-rays, make phone calls, eat, and drink coffee. One wall was lined with bookcases filled with various medical textbooks. A refrigerator, coffee maker, and other odds and ends filled another wall. Windows took up most of a third wall, providing a lovely view of the parking lot, and the final wall displayed the X-ray viewing boxes. You've seen those on TV: rectangular boxes with bright lights in the back. You put the X-ray film on the box, turn on the light, and thoughtfully squint at the film.

When I entered the lounge, I noticed a film hanging on one of the viewing boxes; next to it was an index card with some printing. Immediately, I understood what it was. Or thought I did.

I'd seen these at school: view boxes with hanging X-ray film and an attached index card with the patient's symptoms. Med students would look at the X-ray, review the listed symptoms on the card, and come up with a diagnosis. A week later, the correct diagnosis would be listed, and a new X-ray and history would be up on the box.

I walked over to the unlit X-ray and read the index card:

Patient complained he couldn't sleep at night. The light kept him awake.

I was puzzled. I knew many diseases could cause insomnia, but the thing about the light confused me. If the light kept the patient awake, why didn't he just turn it off? As I mentally scanned the list of diagnoses that might fit, I determined that a tumor inside the patient's brain must be affecting his optic nerves. I therefore expected to see some form of skull X-ray when I turned on the light behind the box.

Instead, to my surprise an X-ray of an abdomen appeared. I recognized the features: bottom parts of lungs and heart, upper thighs, and almost everything in between. I could see a faint outline of the kidneys and liver, plus a number of bones far more distinctive than the less visible internal organs.

It took me a few seconds to review these standard anatomical features, for my attention was focused on something else: something in the patient's rectum that—even to my inexperienced eyes—didn't belong there. A crystal-clear image of a metal flashlight showed up on the X-ray. You could see not just the outer metal shell, but also the light bulb, the on/off switch, the batteries, even the wires. It was one of the most memorable X-ray images I would ever see in my career.

For a minute, I just stood there looking at it intently. I had seen a lot of X-rays as a med student—scans that showed cancers, pneumonia, kidney stones, bowel obstructions, and seemingly endless other types of pathology. But I had never seen anything like this. Eventually, the intern on call for the ER noticed me standing there, staring slack-jawed with what I can only imagine was a look of complete bewilderment. He walked over and stood next to me in front of the X-ray.

"Kinda funny, isn't it?" he said. "Especially the part about the light keeping him awake."

I didn't respond immediately.

"It's a flashlight," I said.

"Yeah." The intern nodded, pursing his lips as he examined the X-ray.

"It's in the patient's rectum."

He looked at me and smiled. "Yeah, we see this," he said nonchalantly, as if to say, *Don't worry, you'll get used to it.*

After staring at the bizarre X-ray for a while, I was wondering what to do next when the ER director walked back into the lounge, pointed at me and said curtly, "You. There's a patient in Room 8. Go examine him."

I didn't bother to ask why.

"Yes sir," I responded briskly, and headed for Room 8.

As I walked down the hallway, my self-assurance started to diminish. My heart pounded, my breathing increased, anxiety nearly overwhelmed me, and I began to perspire profusely. This was what I had been training for the past six years—four years of college and the first two years of medical school. I was about to walk into a room and see a patient, take a history from him, perform a physical exam, then come up with a diagnosis and plan for him. I was about to see a patient who would likely think I was a doctor—unless I messed up badly.

As I stood outside the door to Room 8, I made sure my tie was correctly knotted and its point was directly above my belt buckle. I straightened my white jacket and combed my hair. Satisfied that I looked like a doctor, I confidently entered the room.

Lying on a gurney was a man about 6'6" and 250 pounds—mostly muscle, from what I could tell. I was so nervous and focused on acting like a doctor that I failed to notice that all four appendages were in full leather restraints lashed tightly to the side railings on the gurney. The patient was almost completely immobilized.

Even if I had noticed the restraints, I was so inexperienced that I wouldn't have comprehended what they implied. At this point in my budding career, however, I apparently lacked both experience *and* common sense.

I cleared my throat.

"Good morning, sir. I'm Paul Waymack."

We'd been told that while we were still medical students, we could not introduce ourselves as *Doctor*. If we gave our first and last names while wearing a white lab coat, however, patients would usually assume we were, in fact, doctors.

"What seems to be the trouble?"

My voice was louder and higher than normal due to my extreme nervousness; it probably hadn't sounded like that since puberty. I was embarrassed by the sound of my voice and feared it had conveyed my inexperience and anxiety. I worried the patient would sense the apprehension in my voice and ask if I was really a doctor—one of the worst things you could say to a third-year med student.

The patient, however, said nothing. In fact, he appeared to not even notice I had entered the room.

I quickly contemplated the patient's strange lack of a response. *Why is he ignoring me?* I wondered. *Did he already realize I'm only a med student? What gave me away so quickly?* Anxiety and self-doubt crept in.

Then the light went on—*Aha!* I quickly wrote down on my clipboard, "patient's hearing severely impaired." I smiled, pleased, as I looked down at this notation. Five seconds into my career as a student-physician, and already I had identified an abnormal physical finding!

Flushed with the confidence of having just obtained what I considered a diagnostic coup, I now felt my heart and breathing slow down. Instinctively, I stuck my chest out a bit and cocked my head slightly to the side. I may not have been a doctor yet, but I suddenly believed that strong evidence already showed I was going to be very good at it.

I walked up to the head of the gurney and drew close to the patient's ear. He continued to ignore me as his eyes wandered aimlessly about in the general direction of the ceiling.

"SIR, WHAT SEEMS TO BE THE TROUBLE?" I said in a very loud, authoritative voice.

This time I got a response from the patient, though it was not the one I had expected. Instead of hearing a description of his problems, I was greeted with a bloodcurdling scream. He then struggled forcefully to sit up. As he yanked on the leather restraints, he began to bend one of the metal railings on the gurney and lunged at me, yelling unintelligibly. It was as though Dr. Frankenstein's monster had suddenly come to life, and I was the doctor who had put him there.

My upright and cocky posturing ended instantly. My body was halfway to the fetal position before I regained control, and my pulse increased by at least twenty beats a minute. I backed out of the room as quickly as possible with my eyes constantly focused on the patient in case he broke free. Without thinking, I shouted the number-one most used expression of med students who realize they are in over their heads:

"I'll go get the doctor!"

With that, I left the room and headed back towards the doctors' lounge at a brisk pace. By the time I got there, my jacket was no longer straight and I had loosened my tie and unbuttoned the top button of my shirt.

I found the ER director sipping a cup of coffee and reading some document in his lap. I glanced at him, relieved that he apparently didn't see me enter the lounge. But as soon as I sat down, without removing his eyes from his reading material, he asked the question that's guaranteed to cause anxiety in new third-year medical students.

"So, *Doctor*. What do you think your patient has?" He wasn't exactly smirking, but I knew sarcasm when I heard it.

Only then did it occur to me that I hadn't accomplished every doctor's primary objective: come up with a possible diagnosis. In fact, in my hurried efforts to exit Room 8 with my life intact, I had failed to take any medical history or perform any physical examination of the patient. All I knew was that the patient seemed to be hard of hearing, insane, and preternaturally strong. My mind raced for a diagnosis that would fit those symptoms.

Fortunately, I did not know too many diagnoses at that time, which shortened the amount of time required to contemplate each one. Among the diagnoses I knew was drug abuse.

"Maybe he's on drugs, like amphetamines?" I offered.

The director smiled. "Well that's possible, considering his bizarre behavior, but what about all the perspiring he's doing?"

Perspiring? I thought, stunned. *I was the one doing all the perspiring!*

"Huh?" I responded uncertainly.

The director finally looked up from the paper in his lap and chuckled. Not a good sign.

"With all the perspiration, wouldn't delirium tremors be a more likely diagnosis?" he quizzed.

I paused for a few seconds, trying to appear as though I were thoughtfully contemplating this possibility.

"Oh, yes," I responded casually. "Of course you're correct. DTs is a more likely diagnosis."

"Indeed," he said drily. He then reviewed the consequences of taking alcohol away from addicts.

"DTs include hallucinations, loss of touch with reality, plus many physiologic changes including a rapid pulse and a lot of perspiring," he explained, like a professor patiently lecturing to a class of first-year students. "If not treated, patients can sometimes die from it."

As I listened to him, I vaguely remembered learning about DTs as a second-year. Now that I had actually seen a patient with DTs—especially someone who looked as if he used to play defensive tackle for the Green Bay Packers—I was never going to forget it again.

"So… how do you treat those patients?" I asked the director.

He shrugged.

"Oh, you give them IV fluids to replace what they lose from perspiration, and vitamins—since a lot of these patients have vitamin deficiency due to a diet that has consisted solely of gin and vodka."

My mind remained focused on the patient's wild behavior.

"Yes, but how do you keep them from—well, from attacking us?"

He smiled. "Oh, you give them Librium," he explained. "Twenty-five milligram shots until they calm down."

That was the first drug for which I ever learned the exact dosage—and I never forgot it. By the end of that month, I had also learned that when you work in the ER, you use a great deal of Librium.

I spent the next half-hour reading about DTs, then went off to see a series of sore throats, backaches, and flu cases. These were the kinds of maladies I had expected to see in practice, before the third year of medical school kicked me into reality. But it wasn't long before there were more cases in which patients had been injured doing really stupid things. I wondered how long the craziness would last, and when sanity would return.

One of the nice things about the rotation at Riverside Hospital was that we were never pressured to see patients or stay long hours at the hospital, but were allowed to set our own pace. It was the only rotation with such a schedule for third-year students. I was excited to take advantage of the free time, though, so I ended up staying in the ER until very late. The first night was no exception. I didn't start heading back to my apartment until 11:00 p.m., after the night-shift intern had taken over for his daytime counterpart.

Unfortunately—or fortunately, from the night-shift intern's point of view—it was just at 11:00 when a patient arrived, yelling and screaming as the ambulance crew brought him into the unit. I decided to hang around for a few minutes, since it seemed likely the patient had DTs, and I now knew a lot about those. If that was the case, I could impress everyone on the night shift with my new knowledge, and the intern would, hopefully, give me an outstanding grade on my performance.

As the nurse and intern tried to control the patient, I reached over and touched the skin on the patient's extended arm, looking for perspiration. Upon palpating his skin, however, I found it to be very dry. I determined that this patient was not having DTs; he was merely crazy from amphetamines. *Damn*, I thought. With that, I decided to call it a day and head on back to the apartment.

Meanwhile, the intern and nurse seemed to succeed at least partially in quieting the patient.

The experienced nurse clearly knew what to do next. "Full leather restraints?" she asked. "The usual 25 milligrams of Librium?"

The intern shook his head.

"That won't be necessary," he responded brusquely. "Just get him out of his clothes and into a gown, then send him up to the Psych ward. Let *them* worry about him."

The nurse derisively looked at the cocky intern and rolled her eyes. Convinced that I could learn nothing more from this patient, I went back to the doctor's lounge to pick up the textbook and other items I had brought in that morning. The intern followed me into the lounge, where he began writing an admission note for the patient. The note included orders on how the patient was to be treated: how often to take his vital signs, what to feed him, and what medications to give him.

I wished the intern a good night and was about to leave when the nurse ran into the lounge.

"He just ran off into the parking lot!" she gasped, glaring at the intern. She didn't have to add, "I told you so!"

As we looked out the lounge window, we could see him running past one of the parking lot lights. He was stark naked—the nurse had just managed to get his clothes off before he bolted for freedom.

The intern looked at me and barked, "Come on, we've got to catch him!"

We both ran out the ER doors into the parking lot, chasing after the drug addict. An orderly soon joined us in our unscheduled late-night calisthenics. I knew I had forgotten some things from my first two years of med school, but I was fairly certain none of my professors had ever mentioned catching crazy naked patients in the middle of the night.

The parking lot was enormous, and it was very dark. *That guy sure can run fast*, I thought breathlessly. We spent ten minutes chasing him as he ran between, around, and sometimes over the tops of parked cars. As we ran after him, the intern would holler things such as, "Cut him off at the Pontiac!" Now, that was the type of order I had never dreamed I would be receiving from interns.

Finally, we cornered and tackled him. The patient laid face down on the pavement, shouting and struggling. Trying fiercely to restrain him, I was sitting on his upper back with my knees gripping his head, while the intern was sitting on the back of his thighs, trying not to touch the patient's naked butt that stuck up between us. We looked like we were trying to ride a bull in tandem. Never having been taught how to deal with this situation, I turned around and was about to ask the intern, *Now what?* But when I noticed the uncertain look on his face, I figured we were both clueless.

At that moment in the darkened parking lot, two legs in very white stockings suddenly appeared. The nurse stood over us, smirking.

"So, do you want him to have the Librium?" she asked the intern.

"Uh, yes," he sheepishly answered. "25 milligrams."

With that confirmation, the nurse pulled out a syringe and a vial of

Librium. She drew up the Librium into the syringe, then bent down between the intern and me and wiped the patient's buttock with an alcohol swab. She calmly stabbed it with the syringe, then left to get a gurney.

As the intern and I sat on the patient, waiting for the Librium to take effect, I couldn't resist asking a question. As nonjudgmentally as possible, I asked the intern, "Why did you tell the nurse to not restrain him or give him Librium?"

The intern contemplated that for a few seconds and then said, "Well, at the time it seemed like a reasonable decision."

About ten minutes later, the patient calmed down. The orderly brought out a gurney, the nurse placed a gown on the now-mellow patient, and the orderly wheeled the patient up to the Psych ward.

At this point, I noticed my trousers and white jacket were no longer clean and my shirttail was hanging outside my trousers. After tucking in my shirt and brushing off as much of the dirt from the parking lot as I could, I headed to my apartment.

As I drove, I reflected on what a bizarre day it had been. I figured I would probably practice medicine for well over 10,000 days during my medical career, and yet it would be nearly impossible for any of those subsequent days to be as bizarre as this first day. *What are the odds*, I thought in amazement, *that of all the days I will practice medicine, the most insane will be the first!*

I continued believing this for about nine more hours—until the second day in the ER began as strangely as the first had ended.

A Fistfight
in the ER

O N MY SECOND DAY in the Riverside ER, I got up and—since my best shirt, trousers, and white doctor's coat were now covered with parking lot dirt and oil—put on my second-best shirt, trousers, and tie, as well as a perfectly unstained and unwrinkled white doctor's coat.

Once I reached the hospital, I parked in the main lot. I neatly straightened my coat and tie and walked through the main entrance of the hospital. As I neared the ER, I heard a great deal of noise coming from that side of the hospital. I nervously opened the door to the ER and encountered a scene that looked straight out of a movie: about two dozen people were yelling, screaming, and hitting each other with fists, chairs, tables, and whatever else was available. A couple of doctors and some nurses were trying to maintain some order, but a security guard, who had taken up a position in an unobtrusive corner of the ER, was clearly intent on staying out of the fight.

Having just chased, tackled, and pinned a patient in the ER parking lot nine hours earlier, and since (unlike the doctors, nurses, and security guards) I was not getting paid to do this but rather was *paying* for the privilege of working in the ER, I decided to take a bye on the morning scrimmage. I promptly turned around and headed to the cafeteria, where I had a leisurely breakfast during which I began to consider the possibility that my idyllic image of a physician's career might be woefully out of touch with reality.

Nonetheless, my optimism and naiveté won out over my cynicism, and after breakfast I returned to the emergency room, convinced that I would hear a reasonable explanation.

When I returned to the ER, which had now returned to a more civilized state, I innocently asked, "Anything interesting happening?"

The nurses and interns told me about the fight. Then they told me why it had occurred, but the explanation sounded farfetched—as though it were an implausible plot to a movie or a Shakespearean play.

The story, it seems, was that a young couple had eloped and gotten married the previous year, despite intense objections due to a century-old running feud between the two families. Their love, however, could not be extinguished, and the couple lived blissfully—for at least a year.

Soon they began to bicker, and their passionate arguments escalated. That morning, the wife served the husband burnt toast. It was the last straw in an already precarious marriage. According to the police, the man told his wife he wasn't going to put up with her lousy cooking anymore, so he got his gun and shot her. She arrived by ambulance at the Riverside Hospital ER, where she died within minutes.

Meanwhile, the two families learned about what had happened and both arrived at the ER just before the woman was pronounced dead. Fortunately, the ER had two separate family waiting areas on opposite ends, so the families were, by sheer luck, segregated into the separate waiting areas. Neither family was aware of the other's presence until after they received news of the woman's death, at which point grief and rage merged—which coincided with the two families happening to meet in the middle of the ER. The feud immediately resurrected with increased vigor of such severity that it took numerous policemen to separate them.

After hearing the story, I approached the sole remaining policeman dealing with the paperwork regarding the shooting. Still perplexed, I asked him if the man had given any explanation other than "burnt toast" for shooting his wife. The policeman looked at me before answering, and was experienced enough to recognize that I was not a doctor, but rather a young medical student. He gave me a sympathetic chuckle.

"Well," he recounted, "the guy said he got mad and that shooting her 'just seemed like a good idea at the time.'"

Until that day, I had not been aware of the amount and magnitude of domestic violence in this country. And though I saw much of it in the years that followed, I never grew numb to it.

The next morning when I returned to the ER for my third day, I put on the first trousers and shirt I saw in my closet. And although I put on a tie, I did not notch it up tightly around my neck, and I did not bother buttoning the top button on my shirt. I was beginning to accept reality, and among reality's truths was the fact that nobody in the ER cared how you looked.

Number One

BY THE END OF MY ROTATION at Riverside Memorial Hospital, I was practically an old-timer. I'd had a lot of experience by then, and I was feeling confident and sure-footed.

One day, I was called to the ER to see a patient. On my way in to the exam room, I grabbed the patient's medical chart from the little plastic box on the front of the door. As I put my hand on the door handle, I glanced at the name, age, weight, prior medical conditions, and current symptoms. The chief complaint read: "Having problems with number one." I caught myself before I opened the door.

Number one, I thought, puzzled. *Hmmm.* I had never heard urine referred to as "number one," or feces as "number two." I was familiar with many other euphemisms for bodily fluids, some of which the *New York Times* refuses to print, but not those. Apparently I had some holes in my otherwise comprehensive education and life experiences.

Undeterred, I walked into the room to find an older gentleman ("George") sitting nervously on the examining table. I was used to finding my patients somewhat anxious, but I wasn't sure whether that was because they were concerned that I was their doctor, or because they were worried about their illness. I figured it was probably a combination of both.

I smiled at him brightly.

"Good day, sir. My name is Paul Waymack. What seems to be the problem?"

George cleared his throat.

"I'm having problems with my number one," he said uncomfortably.

Not wanting to show my ignorance, I tried the Socratic method.

"Can you tell me more about these problems?"

"Gets me up at night," he muttered, embarrassed.

Ahhh, I thought, mentally slapping my forehead. *Of course. Number one is his wife!* I smiled at the clever nickname.

"How often?" I questioned, pen poised above my clipboard.

"Most nights."

"Wow," I responded, writing that down.

"Sometimes a couple of times in the same night," he admitted.

I was puzzled. Why was his wife waking him during the night, and why had he come to the ER to tell me? Either the wife was a nymphomaniac— or there was a deeper psychiatric issue at play. A control issue, maybe? A cry for attention? *Perhaps they both need psychiatric help,* I thought. Clearly, George was so hen-pecked he couldn't handle this woman on his own. Having arrived at two possible diagnoses so quickly, I eagerly continued my questioning.

"Have you talked to your wife about this?"

He looked sheepish. "As a matter of fact, I did."

"What did she tell you?"

"She told me to come see you!" George said, shrugging.

Classic avoidance behavior, I thought.

"She didn't say anything else?" I looked up from my clipboard.

He looked at me kind of funny. "No…" he said uncertainly.

"Hmm," I said, pursing my lips. Convinced that a controlling wife was emotionally bullying poor George, I decided to take an alternate tack.

"Well, what do you do after you're awakened?" I expected to hear that he gave in to her sexual demands.

He hesitated, confused by my question.

"Well, I get up and go to the bathroom!" he exclaimed. *Hmm,* I thought. *Severe avoidance on his part as well.* I wrote that down.

"Well, what do you do while you're in the bathroom?" I was determined to get to the root of this strange problem.

By this point, George's expression made it clear that he resented my line of questioning.

"I take a leak," he explained slowly. I couldn't quite read his expression.

"Then what?" I pressed on, expecting him to tell me how long he stayed in the bathroom avoiding his wife before he returned to bed.

"I go back to bed!" he said impatiently.

"Do you say anything to your wife?"

"Well, if she's still awake I apologize for having awakened her." George looked perturbed, as if my questions had nothing to do with his problem.

That he apologized to his wife for her demeaning treatment convinced me this was a classic battered-husband case. I proceeded gently.

"Is there anything you can do in the evening to make it less likely you're awakened?"

He paused for a moment and looked pensive. Then his tone changed from irritation to discovery.

"Well, now that you mention it, it seems that if I don't have any drinks at night, number one doesn't wake me up so much!"

Aha, I thought. *Now I get it. This man has a drinking problem!* I deduced that on the nights George drank excessively, his wife got mad, but passive-aggressively waited until the middle of the night to punish him.

"What does your wife say about your drinking?" I asked.

"She always says I should drink less."

"Have you tried that?"

"No. Do you think I should?"

"Well, drinking to excess is always a bad idea."

"How much is an excess?"

Hmm, I thought. *Should I just be blunt and say don't get drunk, or should I be a little more sensitive?*

"Well, one drink in the evening shouldn't do any harm," I said.

"But that's all I drink most nights!" George exclaimed.

"Are you sure?" I was skeptical.

"Oh yes." He was adamant.

Why, I wondered, would one drink a night upset his wife so much? Both of us were pensive for a moment. Then George looked up hopefully.

"My friend Ed had the same problem," he recalled. "They did an operation on him that fixed the problem."

I couldn't think of anything to say to that. I didn't know what kind of operation Ed could have had, but I knew it couldn't have fixed marital difficulties.

"Oh?" I asked, completely baffled. "What kind of operation?"

The look on George's face said, *What kind of a doctor are you?!*

"You know, a roto-rooter on his prostate."

I knew what a roto-rooter was: slang for surgically reaming out an enlarged prostate. But I couldn't figure out why— *Ohhhhh.* Suddenly the light went on: he had an enlarged prostate that prevented him from fully emptying his bladder, which led to sleep disruptions.

"You okay, Doc?" George asked, not comprehending the look of discovery on my face.

"Just fine, George," I said, waving my hand. "Now let's get back to you telling me how often you urinate at night."

The Chief Resident's Whip

AFTER COMPLETING MY ONE-MONTH ROTATION at Riverside Memorial Hospital, I returned to the Medical College in Richmond to continue my next rotations: one week of ophthalmology, one week of ENT, two weeks of plastic surgery, two months of pediatrics, two months of surgery, six weeks of OB/GYN, six weeks of psychiatry, and finally three months of internal medicine.

Unusually bizarre events were routine that year. I witnessed many of them personally, and fellow med students shared their own incredible experiences at lunch or dinner. The storytelling generally began with "You're not going to believe this." Initially, we didn't. But after a while we reached the point where anything seemed possible—and this was especially the case on surgery rotations.

During my two-month rotation in surgery at the Medical College, one of the very first—and most important—things I learned is that surgeons are frequently arrogant and do not want to be crossed. This is even true of residents. In fact, a surgery chief resident will generally only view an attending surgeon—a med school professor—as his superior. Even internal medicine attendees are cautious about telling a surgery chief resident "no."

One surgery chief resident ("Dr. Collins") was particularly hostile to those who attempted to counter him. (Fortunately, I was not on his rotation, but the students who worked under him shared this story with me.) In the middle of my third year, the five third-year students who were finishing their rotation gave Dr. Collins a fitting farewell gift: a large whip, the type lion tamers use.

As he opened the gift-wrapped package, all the students held their breaths. Would he be offended or pleased? He had both a short fuse and a wicked sense of humor, so no one was sure. Everyone exhaled in relief when they saw his immediate delight. The whip, he said proudly, would add to his reputation as someone not to be crossed. He unstrapped his belt and put it through the coiled whip, letting it hang alongside him like Indiana Jones.

Now appropriately suited up, Dr. Collins began rounds, followed by his tamed group of medical students, interns, and residents.

Due to the hectic nature of a surgery rotation, the attire of surgery residents and students varies widely. Some wear regular street clothes, having had no time to change. Those coming from the OR are wearing scrubs. Some wear white coats over their street clothes or scrubs, and some don't—unlike their colleagues on the internal medicine rotation who always wear perfectly clean white coats. Thus, when one sees a surgery team making rounds, it's perfectly normal to see a motley group of people trotting behind the chief.

That day was no different. When Dr. Collins began rounds with his whip, about half the team was wearing white coats, over a variety of clothes. The team started by checking in with a couple of patients in the prison ward.

The Medical College hospital had 17 floors and was shaped like a cross. On each floor, a nursing station sat in the center of the cross, and the four wings of the cross were patient wards. On one floor, one of the wards was for prisoners from the nearby state penitentiary, the entrance to which was through a locked door guarded by two penitentiary guards. No one could get in or out of the locked ward without the armed guards' approval.

While the other wards only had patients with one type of medical problem—surgery, cardiology, obstetrics, etc.—the prison ward held all prisoners, regardless of the ailment. Thus, a variegated stream of physicians constantly came in and out of the prison ward. However, because all the prisoners wore hospital pajamas, there was little possibility of a prisoner ever exiting through the locked door without the guards noticing.

As Dr. Collins and his team approached the locked door of the prison ward, one of the guards stopped him and demanded the whip. The chief was undeterred and waved them aside.

"I'm the surgery chief resident," he said curtly.

The guard didn't care if he was the president of the United States.

"No weapons inside the prison ward," he said firmly. "That's the policy."

Dr. Collins continued to argue, but the guard wasn't budging. Finally, the chief narrowed his eyes at the guard. He took off the whip, crossly slapped it into the guard's hand, and strode into the ward. None of his team dared say a word.

The chief examined the prisoners without incident. On his way out, he glared at the guard and demanded his whip back.

While the rest of the team headed to the stairwell a few feet away, Dr. Collins held back with a resident wearing street clothes but no white jacket, which was how he had been dressed when he entered the prison ward. The chief reattached the whip to his belt.

As they started to walk towards the stairwell, still within earshot of the guards, Dr. Collins clapped the resident on his shoulder.

"Bob, that was sure nice of you to give that shivering patient your coat." It took a few seconds for the guards to realize the implications of what had just happened. They hightailed it into the ward, searching in vain for a prisoner wearing a white jacket who, if undiscovered, might pass himself off as a doctor and escape.

Dr. Collins, satisfied that his reputation was secure, continued to lead the team in rounds.

An Unusual Rx

A S ONE MIGHT EXPECT, life for a prisoner in the hospital was a lot nicer than in the state penitentiary. The food was better. The beds were more comfortable. The nurses were a lot cuter than the guards. Of course, there were numerous incentives and ways to get one admitted to the hospital, but few inmates were as ingenious as "Butch," who decided to swallow a spoon one day.

Immediately upon swallowing, Butch notified the guards, somewhat inaudibly, of what he had done. At the penitentiary clinic, an X-ray confirmed a full-sized spoon in his stomach. An ambulance quickly dispatched him to the MCV hospital.

The surgery team examined him in the prison ward. Dr. Collins saw two options: wait and see if the spoon passed on its own, or operate. The actual operation would be simple—open the stomach, remove the spoon, close the stomach and abdomen. Since surgery interns—lower than the residents but higher than us med students—almost never get to operate inside the abdomen, Dr. Collins turned to one of the interns on his team.

"Do you want to open him up and take out the spoon?"

Delighted, the intern scrubbed for surgery and, with the chief's assistance, surgically removed the spoon. Butch had an uneventful postoperative course and was sent back to the penitentiary about 10 days later.

Back in the cell, Butch gave the other prisoners a glowing account of his vacation in the hospital, which was well worth the discomfort of the surgery. Unsurprisingly, within a few days several other prisoners swallowed spoons and were sent to MCV.

The surgery interns greatly enjoyed performing the operations, but eventually the stream of spoon-swallowing prisoners became ridiculous, and Dr. Collins determined to put an end to this waste of taxpayers' money.

Following completion of any operation, the surgeon always writes a series of orders for the nurses. The orders include such things as how frequently to monitor the patient's vital signs (pulse, blood pressure, temperature, and respiratory rate), dietary restrictions, and medications protocol.

As the intern began writing orders for the latest spoon-swallowing prisoner, Dr. Collins asked what pain medications he intended to prescribe.

"Demerol," the intern responded, assuming this was a quiz. A powerful narcotic usually prescribed post-operation, Demerol is given by injection.

"Nope," Dr. Collins answered.

"Morphine injections?"

"Nope."

The intern gave up.

"What should I prescribe?"

"Tylenol suppositories every six hours as needed," the chief said.

The intern furrowed his brow in confusion. He hesitated, knowing how the chief didn't take kindly to challenges.

"Umm, suppositories?" he questioned. "But that won't even begin to control his pain."

Dr. Collins shrugged his shoulders and left the OR.

The intern dutifully wrote an order for Tylenol suppositories, 650 mg every six hours as needed. When the nurse saw the order, her eyes bugged out.

"What are you thinking?!" she exclaimed, aghast. She handed him back the clipboard. "That's the silliest order I've ever seen!"

Nurses aren't afraid of speaking their minds to lowly interns and med students.

The intern shrugged, handing back the order.

"I'm thinking I'd better do what the chief said to do," he responded sensibly.

Thus, for the next 10 days the recovering prisoner moaned unrelentingly, bitterly complaining of a pain unrelieved by rectal suppositories.

After that, no more spoon-swallowing patients showed up at MCV. At least, not while I was there.

Don't Eat
My Food

O NE DAY DURING MY SURGERY ROTATION, a nurse shared a rather alarming misadventure involving one of the junior residents, who was famous for his eating habits. Specifically, he was known for eating everyone else's food. This was especially a problem in the surgical intensive care unit. Every evening he would enter the nurses' lounge adjacent to the ICU, and eat whatever food was in sight. Generally, he would ask if it was okay to eat the particular item just as it was entering his mouth. If the nurse said no, he would swallow and ask if she wanted it back.

This behavior so appalled one nurse, she decided to teach him a lesson. Knowing the resident loved chocolate, nurse Shelly made a large chocolate cake, and into the batter added a large amount of Ex-Lax.

No longer available in the United States, Ex-Lax was popular in the 1970s as an extremely powerful laxative. It was packaged as chocolate wafers, so when crumbled up and added to a chocolate cake, it was virtually unnoticeable.

The plan was to leave the chocolate cake in the nurses' lounge, and warn everyone but the food-stealing resident. One piece of the cake contained a sufficient quantity of Ex-Lax to ensure severe diarrhea within a few hours.

Unfortunately, the plan went awry. No sooner had Shelly set the cake down prominently in the center of the nurses' lounge than she was called to an emergency in the radiology department, where one of the ICU patients had become critically unstable while undergoing some diagnostic tests. Shelly remained stuck in the radiology department for a couple of hours with the deathly ill patient, unable to return to the ICU to warn the other nurses and medical personnel.

Meanwhile, many surgery residents passed through the nurses' lounge in the Surgical ICU, noticed the cake, and asked if they could have a piece. The other nurses, assuming it was up for grabs, told the residents they could each have a slice, so long as they left one for Nurse Shelly.

Eventually, she made it back to the ICU, and was horrified to see that most of her cake had been consumed. To her further dismay, Shelly learned that although most of the surgery residents had eaten a piece, her intended target was not one of them.

That evening, one by one the surgery residents became violently sick with diarrhea. This was inconvenient for most of the residents, but especially for those in the OR, who fought the urge to run to the bathroom until it was almost too late. After hearing the story, I was pleased I had not ventured into the nursing station that evening.

Although no lasting harm was done, Nurse Shelly was reprimanded. I doubt she regretted the incident too much, though. The food-stealing surgery resident, duly paranoid, immediately ceased eating other people's food.

Kunta Kinte

IN FEBRUARY 1977, I started my rotation with the obstetrics and gynecology (OB/GYN) service at the Medical College. During those months, I spent a lot of time in the labor and delivery suite, watching and assisting in births. The OB/GYN rotation was one of the easier ones for a third-year medical student because there were two shifts, and unlike other rotations, med students worked one or the other, but not both. I was initially assigned to the day shift, and spent much of my time in clinic.

Next came two weeks on the night shift. I would arrive at the hospital at 5:00 p.m., attend a lecture from 5:00 to 6:00, then work in the labor and delivery suite until 6:00 a.m., at which time I was relieved by the day shift. I'd go back to my apartment, get some breakfast, read a bit, sleep for a few hours, then head back to the hospital by 5:00 p.m. and start the cycle over.

Med students on rotations had minimal time for social interactions; even finding time to read a newspaper was a rare event. We certainly didn't have the luxury of watching TV on the OB/GYN rotation, because at any given time about a dozen women were in labor at the hospital, and an average of sixteen babies were born every day—not unusual for an inner-city hospital.

My first delivery was thrillingly uncomplicated. After cleaning the blood and amniotic fluid off a robust baby boy, I used a bulb syringe to suck mucus out of his nose so he could breathe easier. He let out a huge squall, and I finally let out a sigh of relief. Nothing had gone wrong.

Beaming with pride, I handed the baby over to his exhausted mother.

"Congratulations, Mrs. Jones!" I exclaimed. "You have a healthy baby boy! Do you have a name for him?"

At the time, Virginia state law required a mother to name her baby soon after delivery, and the attending doctor wrote the name on the birth certificate.

Mrs. Jones, who was even more relieved than I to have the birthing process over, looked blissfully at me while she held her baby.

"Yes," she said serenely. "His name is Kwrk."

Perplexed, I responded, "Querk?"

"Kwrk," she said firmly, correcting me.

Only minutes before, I had been so pleased with myself for successfully bringing my first baby into the world.

"I'm sorry," I said, embarrassed. "Could you tell me how to spell that?"

Mrs. Jones lifted one eyebrow in skepticism.

"If you's can't spell, how did you's gets to be a doctor?!"

The third-year resident who had been observing the delivery felt sorry for me, and motioned for me to follow him out into the hallway. Intuiting that I hadn't had much time in the last couple of years to keep abreast of societal trends, he helpfully explained that the current vogue when naming babies, especially boys, was to make up new names. Yes, some of them even lacked vowels.

For the next several days, through dozens of deliveries and birth certificates, I made a valiant effort to follow the rules of spelling as taught by my fourth-grade teacher, Ms. Hardy. And, having learned from my first experience with Mrs. Jones, I never questioned a new mother's choice of names. Thus, when one patient named her baby "Wock," I didn't miss a beat. When another gave me the name "Talak," I wrote it down phonetically. Only rarely did I hear names I recognized, like "Michael" or "Ellen."

After one delivery during my second week on the night shift, I asked the new mother if she had picked out a name for her baby boy. She was cradling the baby in her arms, cooing at him.

"Yes," she said proudly, looking up. "Kunta Kinte."

"Ah, very good!" I replied, pleased at the wealth of vowels. I dutifully wrote Kunta Kinte on the birth certificate at the physician's desk, and headed back to the labor room.

A few hours and several deliveries later, another patient gave birth to a baby boy. When I asked her if she had picked out a name, the woman didn't hesitate.

"Yes!" she said with shining eyes. "Kunta Kinte."

I had heard many unusual names during my two-week stint on the obstetric service, but I had never heard the same unusual name twice. It didn't seem possible that two women, unrelated to each other, could pull the same unique name out of thin air on the same night!

Puzzled, I glanced down at the admission sheet. *Aha*, I thought. My patient had been admitted late that afternoon, which meant that she and the mother of the other Kunta Kinte had been in the labor suite at the same time. It made sense now—I figured one of them made up the name, and the other mother liked it and decided to use it, too.

At 6:00 a.m. my shift ended. I drove back to my apartment, got a bite to eat, read a chapter from the OB/GYN textbook, and fell fast asleep. I awakened at four o'clock, ate a quick lunch, and returned to the hospital. When I got up to Labor & Delivery, another third-year med student was delivering a baby. I stayed in the labor suite, observing the miraculous process.

"Congratulations, Mrs. Andrews!" exclaimed the student, handing the cleaned-up baby over to the mother. "What a beautiful baby boy. Do you have a name for him?"

"Yes," the woman said, her face filled with pride and joy. "Kunta Kinte."

I only had a few seconds to ponder this Twilight Zone coincidence before a woman in labor arrived, her cervix fully dilated. We barely had enough time to get her into the delivery suite before a healthy baby boy popped out.

I handed the squealing infant over to his beaming mother, along with my enthusiastic congratulations. Somewhat cautiously, I queried whether she had picked out a name for him.

"Oh yes," she said. "Kunta Kinte!"

I just had to ask.

"Oh, that's such an interesting name! How did you come up with it?"

She raised an eyebrow and looked at me skeptically, as if she were wondering how I got to be a doctor. I glanced at the resident, who was no help.

Thankfully, the nurse in the delivery suite was more up to date on popular culture than we were.

"Roots!" she said, laughing, after the mother returned to her room. "The

name's from *Roots.*"

The resident and I remained confused. Vegetable roots? Tree roots? We looked at her blankly.

"It was on last month! Don't you guys ever watch TV?" she asked.

"Actually, no." Neither of us had in some time. The nurse patiently explained that *Roots* was a show that had been on TV every night for a week in January, and the main character was an African slave named Kunta Kinte. None of that rang the faintest bell, although I later learned that 130 million Americans had watched the show.

I doubt that number included any med students.

I have since often wondered what happened to all those Kunta Kintes born in February 1977. With African-American history finally getting some attention, it's understandable that many parents would jump at the chance to show their racial pride. Still, I'm sure it made for a confusing first day of kindergarten, five years later.

Schizophrenia and Sexual Neuroses

AFTER COMPLETING MY SIX WEEKS on the OB/GYN rotation, I moved on to my six weeks in the psychiatry service at the Medical College. I was enthusiastic about this rotation, since I had started med school with the plan to be either a psychiatrist or an internal medicine specialist.

For some reason, the psychiatry department thought I had potential. Thus, they gave me one of the prime slots for third-year students: my own office in psychiatry clinic where I would see five patients a day, four days a week. The other third-years had more standard hospital ward rotations.

When I entered my office that first Monday, I was excited to begin a long career in treating patients with psychiatric problems. By chance—or maybe it was fate—all five of my patients that first day were suffering from severe depression. For some of them, the depression was due to outside events such as family tragedies or financial setbacks. For others, the depression was due to an internal problem: a biochemical imbalance in their brain's metabolism. I listened to each patient for an hour, and all of them recounted in detail the many things that were wrong with their lives.

By the end of that first day, I found myself severely depressed. That evening, everything seemed hopeless to me. I was convinced life was not worth living. I have rarely been so depressed during my entire life.

The next day I saw five new patients, four of whom were suffering from paranoid schizophrenia. During my second year in med school, one of the staff psychiatrists had told us that he could always differentiate between a schizophrenic patient and a neurotic patient within the first five minutes of speaking with the patient. If the psychiatrist felt like he wanted to vomit, the patient was schizophrenic. If he had an erection, the patient was sexually neurotic.

I discovered the psychiatrist had not been joking.

Most of this second day in the psychiatry clinic, I felt severely nauseated while seeing these patients. Each patient told me rambling, bizarre tales that all shared the same theme: the world was plotting against them. I heard incredible stories of the government spying on patients, of devices implanted in their brains to control them, even of aliens trying to dominate them. My nausea grew as the day progressed, then my skin began to itch. By that afternoon, I fought the overwhelming desire to bolt from my office.

As I headed home, I found myself repeatedly looking over my shoulder. That evening, I kept nervously glancing out the apartment windows. Never before in my life had I felt so paranoid.

The following day I again saw five new patients. This time, four of them were suffering from severe neuroses. Each of them told me of their unusual, bizarre, and intense sexual needs, desires, and experiences. By noon, I was loosening my tie and unintentionally aroused. Indeed, the psychiatrist's gauge for diagnosing a neurotic patient was accurate.

After each patient completed his hour with me, I prayed that the next would be depressed or psychotic: anything but another patient with more sexually neurotic rants. Yet as the day continued, men and women told me exceptionally vivid sexually neurotic stories and dreams.

As I headed home after a day with these patients, I wasn't sure whether I needed a stiff drink or a tranquilizer. For most of that evening my efforts at reading were thwarted by my hyper-aroused state, and I began to understand that my rotation on the psychiatry service was not going at all according to plan.

The following Monday, my five depressed patients returned for their weekly clinic visit, and that evening I again became severely depressed. The next day I saw my schizophrenic patients, and that evening I again found myself paranoid. Then came Wednesday and my trip to the world of sexual arousal and neuroses.

After six weeks of this emotional roller coaster, I was greatly relieved to move on to the internal medicine rotation. Surely, I thought, my patients would be normal there.

The Spanish-American War Veteran

MY FIRST TWO MONTHS on the internal medicine service were at the Veterans Administration (VA) hospital in Richmond: one month on the gastrointestinal service and one month on the pulmonary service. On the former, we mostly diagnosed patients with bleeding ulcers and gastrointestinal cancers, then transferred them to the surgery service to fix the problem. On the pulmonary service, we also transferred patients to the surgery service, where surgeons biopsied tumors and removed cancerous lungs.

As this transfer process kept repeating itself, I began to realize that surgeons had the most adventurous and decisive roles in medicine. (Not coincidentally, surgery had the longest and most stressful residency, followed by the most stressful career.)

Although I had entered med school thinking I wanted to be either a psychiatrist or a doctor of internal medicine, the excitement of the surgery rotation was alluring. Some have described surgery as "the purest form of medicine," since it separates the disease from the patient. Instead of giving the patient medicine to try to cure the disease, the surgeon cuts the patient open and literally removes the disease.

I wanted to be a surgeon.

Having made that decision, my final two months on the internal medicine service seemed awfully boring compared to surgery. Since this was 1977, before managed care stepped in, we admitted a lot of patients who weren't really all that sick. During this month, the chief complaints of most patients were fatigue and vague aches and pains. In fact, only two patients in this rotation were particularly memorable.

When I arrived at the hospital one morning, a fellow third-year regaled me with the story of a patient who had been admitted the night before.

At the time, a unique policy allowed Spanish-American War veterans to be admitted to the hospital for any reason, even if the vet had no medical needs. Since the war was fought in 1898, any veteran still alive had to be well into his nineties, so the policy seemed reasonable and compassionate—you know, put a roof over their heads for the night and give them a couple of square meals.

One night, an aging veteran showed up at the VA in Richmond, complaining of various aches and pains. The ER doctors noted that the only thing wrong with him seemed to be that he was cold and hungry, but since the man said he was a Spanish-American War veteran, they admitted him. The following morning, one of the internal medicine doctors examined him, and after confirming that he had no medical ailment, released him. This happened multiple times, although none of his stays ever lasted more than about twelve hours.

One cold night, the veteran showed up at the VA, but this time the ER doctor found that he was truly ill with pneumonia. He was sent to the internal medicine ward and started on antibiotics. The following morning when the veteran was not discharged, his name turned up in the administrator's office, along with a note that he needed a VA card.

It turned out that—due to several convoluted reasons having to do with administrative bureaucracy—the hospital never received confirmation from the Veterans Administration that this man had been honorably discharged from military service. Consequently, he had never received a VA card allowing him unfettered access to hospital services.

At this point, a series of communications ensued between the Richmond VA hospital and the Veterans Administration headquarters in Washington, D.C. A concise summary:

Hospital: "But he swears he's a Spanish-American War veteran! He's given us his dates of service!"

VA Headquarters: "But we don't have any record of him having served! Are you sure he's given you the right name?"

After a lengthy investigation, the VA discovered that the veteran indeed had been telling the truth. He did fight in the Spanish-American War... but with the *Spanish* Army. It never occurred to any of the doctors or VA administrators to ask the man, "Whose side did you fight on?"

The poor fellow wasn't trying to cheat anyone. He had simply heard that all Spanish-American War veterans were entitled to an overnight stay at the VA hospital. And since he was such a veteran, as well as an American citizen for about forty years, he figured he might as well take advantage of the free room and board.

King Kong

I SAW THE SECOND MEMORABLE PATIENT on the internal medicine service on a Sunday afternoon, when I was back at the Medical College hospital in downtown Richmond. Before entering her room, I grabbed her admission sheet that noted she was seventy years old and complained of lethargy. I sighed, knowing that I'd spend the next half-hour doing a history and physical examination of a patient who was probably just depressed from getting old.

Come on, I thought, trying to cheer myself up. *In a few weeks you'll be back to taking care of patients with interesting diseases that can be fixed with an operation.*

With that happy thought in my mind, I smiled and entered the patient's room.

"Good afternoon, Mrs. Smith," I said brightly. "So what brings you to the hospital today?"

"My son brought me here in his car!" She laughed at her clever joke, as though she were the first one to think of it.

I smiled patiently.

"Was it a nice drive?"

"Oh, yes. Especially seeing King Kong on top of the building!"

Today, you might have assumed that she had watched a video of *King Kong* in the car—but in 1977, there weren't even video players in homes. I figured she had just gone to a theater. The monster thriller movie with Jessica Lange and Jeff Bridges had come out the year before and was still very popular.

"Oh? You went to the movies today?"

"No, I saw him on top of a tall building while my son was driving me here. Didn't you see him?"

I had learned in my second year of medical school that people who hear voices when no one is around are likely paranoid schizophrenics. However, patients who *see* things that aren't there are likely on drugs and hallucinating.

I cocked my head and looked at Mrs. Smith quizzically. She didn't seem like the type to take LSD.

"Do you know why he's up there?" she asked.

"Umm, well, I don't actually know. Just how big was he?"

She looked up at the ceiling and pursed her lips, as though trying to gauge the height.

"Oh, at least twenty feet tall."

Wow, I thought. Clearly, she was a few tacos short of a combination plate.

"Do you know how he got up to the top of the building?" she queried. "It must be at least twelve stories high."

"I don't, sorry," I responded. "What exactly does he look like?"

She shrugged.

"Oh, just a twenty-foot-tall gorilla."

I moved on.

"Let's talk about the fatigue you've been experiencing. Can you tell me when that first started?"

Except for the giant gorilla story, she seemed like a typical seventy-year-old widow who was depressed because she didn't have her husband around. She hadn't taken any drugs that could have caused the hallucination.

I performed a complete physical exam, then walked out to the nurses' station and sat down with a blank report in front of me. I couldn't decide how to put this case down on paper. As I considered the various possible diagnoses, I overheard two orderlies down the desk from me.

"What's it doing on top of that building?" one asked.

"Yeah. But my question is, *how* did they get it to the top of that building?"

Eventually, I learned that a magazine publisher had decided to generate publicity by putting a twenty-foot-tall model of King Kong on top of a high-rise with a crane, causing one helluva distraction in downtown Richmond.

I also learned that when patients tell you crazy things, sometimes they're true.

The Calm
Before the Storm

MY FOURTH YEAR OF MEDICAL SCHOOL, happily, was comprised entirely of electives. Having decided to become a surgeon, I spent that year exclusively on various surgical services for the first half of the year: vascular, general, cardiac, and pediatric surgery. I was on call only once every four nights, worked a reasonable number of hours, and still had time to interview for residencies.

I spent the second half of the year in the experimental surgical research lab at MCV, during which I was able to go home every evening. Steve Crute, the research technician for the chairman of surgery, taught me valuable surgical skills by operating on dogs. He also regaled me with stories of experiments gone bad. Despite hearing of these fiascos, I nevertheless eventually pursued a career in surgical research.

Thinking of that final year of medical school brings back happy memories. I had survived four years of college while maintaining a near straight-A average, followed by the intellectual, physical, and emotional challenges of the first three years in medical school. Especially compared to the insanity of third-year rotations, my fourth year was blissfully relaxed.

It was merely the calm before the storm.

Part II
The Intern
1978-1979

The 700-Pound Patient

AFTER GRADUATING FROM MEDICAL SCHOOL in June 1978, I left Virginia and headed north for my one-year surgery internship at the Penn State University School of Medicine in Hershey, Pennsylvania.

I thought med school had been isolating, but at Penn State I was virtually sequestered—all surgery interns and residents were expected to work more than one hundred hours per week. We worked every other night on call: a thirty-six-hour shift followed by twelve hours off, then another thirty-six-hour shift, and so on. I was constantly on my feet, running from one critical patient to another. We had on-call sleep rooms at the hospital, but actual sleep tended to be very rare.

Fatigue was my perpetual companion during that year.

When my thirty-six-hour shifts ended, I would stagger back to my apartment, have a quick bite to eat, then crawl into bed. About eight hours later I'd get up, shower and dress, then return to the hospital for my next shift. As in med school, I never had time to watch TV or read a newspaper. This was especially true during my three months on the cardiac surgery service, where my only source of information beyond what happened on my service was an occasional dinner at the hospital with residents from the general surgery service. That's how I found out about a rather unique patient who had been in the news.

The Hershey Medical Center had just started a comprehensive surgical weight-loss program—ironic, since Hershey is the chocolate capital of the U.S. The program included a new surgical procedure to shorten the digestive tract, referred to as an "intestinal bypass." One of the first patients in that program, a woman who weighed more than 700 pounds, was admitted while I was an intern on the cardiac surgery service. Because the scales at the hospital only went up to 350, the doctors had to take the patient down to the loading dock, where they weighed her on the freight scales.

The bariatric surgery was a challenge, to put it lightly. First, a 700-pound patient is far too big to fit on a single operating table, so hospital engineers had to bolt two tables together. The next challenge was adequately scrubbing her belly with the standard antiseptic soap, Betadine scrub. This is normally a simple procedure, but crucial; an inadequate scrubbing can leave bacteria on the skin and predispose the development of a bacterial infection in the wound. According to the resident who scrubbed the patient, it was like trying to scrub the ocean. Each time he would rub the Betadine brush across her belly, waves of fat ripples splattered soap everywhere. The usual five-minute scrub felt like it went on for an hour.

Once the scrubbing was finished, the operation finally began. From what I heard, it was a nightmare. Even under normal circumstances, it's not easy to tie suture knots tightly and securely, since the weight of the tissues tend to untie the knots while the surgeon is trying to tie them. With this patient, the excess weight made the process exceptionally challenging. Exacerbating the tricky situation, the surgeons had to push their gloved hands down into the patient's belly, through a foot of abdominal fat, to get to the stomach. Greased gloves made it impossible to get any traction on the suture the surgeons tried to tie.

To compensate, the surgeons would remove their hands from the patient's belly and attempt to wipe the grease off with a sterile towel. Even when this worked, the grease would reappear when they slid their hands back down into her belly.

According to the interns on this service, the operation set the record for the most number of curses in a single elective case.

Following an operation of this magnitude, it is not unusual for the patient to remain attached to the breathing machine for a few hours or even days if there are problems. Doctors refer to this as being "on the ventilator," and the goal for such patients is to get them off. You do this by slowly decreasing the rate at which the ventilator breathes, and allow the patient to increase the amount of breathing she does on her own.

For a couple of days, the doctors slowly tried to have the patient take over the work of breathing, with no success. Of course, weaning a patient off the ventilator is much easier if she can get out of bed and sit up. The problem was how to get a very heavy patient out of bed when she can't do it herself.

After some thoughtful discussion, the doctors decided to get a consultation from experts who specialize in moving 700-pound patients: equine veterinarians. Resourcefully, the doctors called the nearest vet school in Pennsylvania. I could just imagine the conversation.

Doc:	Say, do you have any horse surgeons over there?
School:	Sure do. Hold on a sec.
	Goes to find vet.
Vet:	Hey there! What can I do for you?
Doc:	We've got a big patient here at the medical center. How do you lift your horses?
Vet:	Well, I put a sling under it, then I connect the sling to a lift above it. Then I crank up the sling and slide the horse over to the operating table.
Doc:	Okay... so what kind of lift are we talking about?
Vet:	You know those engine lifts you find in an auto shop? Just like that.

The Medical Center lacked these resources, but not ingenuity. The doctors asked the veterinarians to send a horse sling by overnight delivery. Next, they called the auto shop down the street from the hospital and asked if they did consultations on designing engine lifts for patients. It turned out that, no, the mechanics had never done medical consultations before, but they were pleased to have the opportunity. After all, it gave them a chance to answer "So what did you do at the garage today, honey?" with a very interesting story.

The auto shop sent over a team. After the mechanics completed their consultation, the hospital engineers hooked up three steel I-beams. One was placed vertically just to the left of the patient's double bed (two regular hospital beds bolted together). They put a wide sofa with a tall armrest on the right side of the bolted beds, then placed the second I-beam vertically on the right of the sofa. Finally, they used a soldering iron to weld a third I-beam horizontally to the tops of the other two.

The hospital rented an engine lift from the garage and mounted it on the horizontal I-beam. When the horse sling arrived, hospital staff worked together to slide it under the patient, then attached the ends to the engine lift. One of the doctors began cranking the lift, and the patient slowly started to hover above the bed. Predictably, she became disconnected from the ventilator.

The anesthesiology resident was standing by with an Ambu bag, a hand-held rubber balloon-type device that forces air down the patient's windpipe into the lungs. On that day, the anesthesiology resident happened to be a five-foot-two, 102-pound woman. She was no match for the patient.

As the engine lift began moving the patient laterally toward the sofa, the anesthesiologist tried to ventilate the patient with both hands around the Ambu bag, while at the same time navigating the distance between the beds and sofa as the lift continued moving. She stumbled backwards over various medical devices while struggling to keep the bag over the patient's mouth.

Eventually, the engineers lowered the patient onto the large sofa, where the tall armrest kept her in a semi-reclined position. Once they removed the sling, the staff reconnected her to the ventilator.

Meanwhile, on the opposite side of the ICU, a patient who'd had open-heart surgery the previous day was watching the horse-lift maneuver with fascination. In fact, everyone in the ICU was watching the proceedings, including the nurse who was supposed to be monitoring her open-heart-surgery patient's heart rate. As this patient watched the move, he became so nervous that his heart began to beat irregularly. His nurse only noticed when the heart monitor urgently started beeping.

By the time of the next move two hours later—from sofa back to bed—

the hospital staff had instituted two new rules regarding the moving of 700-pound patients. One, the anesthesiologist in charge of ventilating the patient during the move had to be at least six feet tall. Two, curtains had to be drawn around all other patients' beds, so they did not become unduly excited.

A Ghost Hospital

ON THE LAST MONDAY IN MARCH, I began my final week on the cardiac surgery service. My euphoria at finishing a brutal rotation was enhanced by my delight that the next rotation was in the ER, which had the easiest schedule—twelve-hour shifts for six consecutive days, then a luxurious three days off. May and June would be my rotation on plastic surgery, which was the second easiest schedule—on call every other night, but plastic surgery patients generally aren't very sick, and I could sleep at the hospital.

A few days before finishing my cardiac surgery rotation—Wednesday, March 28, 1979, to be exact—I took a document to the surgery office. I was concerned when I saw one of the two secretaries ("Doris") looking extremely anxious, so I asked the other secretary ("Mabel") if she knew what was wrong.

"Well," said Mabel in a low whisper, "she's worried about getting radiation poisoning from that nuclear plant."

"Nuclear plant?" I responded with a surprised look. "There's a nuclear power plant nearby?"

Mabel looked incredulous at my ignorance.

"Paul! How long have you been here? Don't you ever watch the news??"

I'd had more than a few people ask me that since I started med school. The answer was always, "No. If I have free time, I sleep."

Mabel pointed at the window.

"There's a nuclear plant just six miles thataway. Haven't you heard about the problem this morning?"

I laughed. After having survived my three months on cardiac surgery, it was going to take more than some minor problem at a nearby power plant to bother me. In fact, I was in such a good mood that I decided to play a little practical joke. I walked down to the radiology department and asked to borrow two of their lead aprons, the ones they wear when they're taking an X-ray.

The radiology technician looked a little curious, but gave them to me without asking any questions. I returned to the surgery office, but before entering I put one of the aprons on in front, and the other covering my back. I opened up the door and walked in, trying to suppress a smile. Both secretaries looked up.

"I hear the reactor just went critical," I said solemnly. "But I'm not worried." I slowly turned around while patting both lead aprons.

Doris jumped up from her desk and ran out of the office in hysterics.

Mabel shook her head and rolled her eyes.

"Paul, it isn't funny," she said. "I think they may have a real problem."

I was about to ask her what had happened when I was paged. Another critically ill cardiac surgery patient needed me in the ICU.

Twenty-six hours later, my shift finally ended. I staggered back to my apartment, bleary-eyed. I was about to collapse in bed when I remembered what Mabel had said, so I turned on the TV just in time to catch the evening news.

I was surprised to learn that Mabel was right.

Walter Cronkite on CBS News was telling America that the partial nuclear meltdown that had occurred at Three Mile Island on Wednesday was releasing radioactive gases and iodine into the environment. Schools were closed and residents were told to stay indoors. Farmers kept their animals under cover and on stored feed. Pennsylvania's governor, Dick Thornburgh, advised the evacuation of pregnant women and young children within a five-mile radius of the power plant.

I guess I should have been as terrified as Doris had been, but between my ongoing exhaustion and the euphoria of knowing that I was two days away from finishing my cardiac surgery rotation, even a meltdown at a nearby nuclear power plant didn't faze me. How bad could it be? Life still went on.

But the next day—Friday, March 30—Governor Thornburgh extended the evacuation orders to a twenty-mile radius, and we spent the day moving patients to more distant hospitals. By nighttime, over ninety percent of the Medical Center's patients had been sent to other hospitals east of us.

I was beginning to think I had been a little too cavalier about the incident.

By Saturday morning, 140,000 people had evacuated the area. Only two patients remained on the cardiac surgery service: two women who were too critical to be transported. I was on call, but since I only had two patients, I managed to grab a couple of hours of sleep.

On Sunday morning, while President Jimmy Carter and Governor Thornburgh were touring the control room at Three Mile Island, the cardiac surgery team made rounds on the two patients, which took all of ten minutes. In the afternoon—with just a few minutes for the transition—I left cardiac surgery and headed down to the ER to start my rotation.

I met the other two members of the ER staff—a second-year resident and a psych intern—and the attending ER physician gave us a quick orientation.

"Shifts run from 8:00 a.m. to 8:00 p.m., then 8:00 p.m. to 8:00 a.m.," he said. "Dr. Waymack, you're taking the night shift first."

I nodded. After three months on the cardiac surgery service, this sounded like a vacation.

The ER attending beckoned us to follow him, and took us outside to the ER entrance. He pointed to a hose attached to a water faucet behind a large bush.

"If the worst happens at Three Mile Island," he said, "the victims will be brought to our ER. We're the closest hospital. It's crucial you hose them off before they're brought in, or the medical center will be contaminated."

The three of us nodded soberly.

"Any questions?"

I had a few, like *Just how severe are things at the reactor? Are we talking hundreds of victims, or thousands? Will we be contaminated by treating them?*

We shook our heads.

"Good," he said briskly. "Oh, by the way, I have to go take care of a family situation in Vermont. I'll be gone for a few days. Good luck!"

With that cheery farewell, he headed off to the parking lot, and we were on our own. Three new doctors to staff the ER—in the middle of a nuclear crisis.

I walked home to my apartment a block away and, for an unprecedented second time in a week, watched the six o'clock news. Even Walter Cronkite's avuncular, reassuring voice couldn't mask the severity of the situation. In light of the apocalyptic possibilities, the ER attending's decision to flee to Vermont seemed quite reasonable.

Nevertheless, I chose to stay in Hershey and man the ER.

I turned off the TV when Cronkite said good night and walked back to the hospital. In the doctors' lounge, I found the psychiatry intern reading a textbook.

"How are things going?" I asked her. "Do you have any patients to sign out to me?"

She gave me a warm smile and got up.

"None at all! I've hardly seen a patient all afternoon. I'm actually kind of pleased about that, since I've spent the last nine months taking care of just psych patients. I was afraid if a patient with a medical problem arrived, I might not know what to do."

"I'm sure you would've done just fine," I assured her.

The intern grabbed her things and left, and I was in charge. *How could there be no patients in the ER at eight o'clock on a Sunday evening?* I wondered. I walked down the hallway, glancing into each of the patient rooms. They were indeed all empty. The full magnitude of the evacuation of the surrounding area was beginning to dawn on me.

I returned to the doctors' lounge and began reading a surgery textbook. Two hours later, still no patients. I turned off the light in the lounge and laid down on the couch. I was asleep as soon as I closed my eyes.

I couldn't have been out for long before the lights flipped on and the night shift nurse was gently shaking my shoulder.

"Dr. Waymack, there's a patient to see you. He says he's suffering from radiation poisoning from Three Mile Island."

Oh my God, I thought. *It's happened! The nuclear core meltdown has destroyed the reactor's containment building, and radiation is streaming out over Pennsylvania.*

I leaped up from the couch, my heart racing.

"What room is he in?!" I demanded, grabbing my white coat.

"Room 1," she said calmly, following me as I bolted out of the lounge. "Would you like to see his old chart before you see him?"

The question seemed ridiculous. What possible use would I have for his old chart? What did it matter if he'd had an appendectomy or pneumonia? None of that had any relevance to his current condition. If he was now coated with radioactive debris from Three Mile Island, my number-one priority was to hose him off.

Then I remembered that first night as a third-year med student in the ER at Riverside Memorial Hospital, when I watched the intern foolishly ignore a nurse's suggestion.

"Certainly," I said, using a respectful tone. I stopped in the hallway outside Room 1.

She smiled. "I'll wheel it in."

I thought that was curious. The nurse soon returned, pushing a cart with several volumes of medical records.

I picked up the top volume. The patient was currently twenty-five years old. The diagnosis from his first ER admission, some years earlier, was paranoid schizophrenia. I opened up several other volumes of his old medical record, and found that all prior hospitalizations resulted in the same diagnosis. I gathered that the incident at Three Mile Island had simply exacerbated his paranoia.

In Room 1, I found a very nervous patient rubbing his hands together.

"Good evening," I said pleasantly. "I'm Dr. Waymack. What seems to be the problem?"

"They're poisoning me!" he said, agitated. "It's all a government plot. They're destroying the reactor to poison me." He continued vigorously rubbing his hands together.

"Do you work at Three Mile Island?" I asked, taking notes.

"No. I'm in between jobs."

"Oh. Why do you think you have radiation poisoning?"

"They told me so!" The patient was becoming frantic.

"Who told you so?"

"The voices!"

"Was anyone else around when these voices said you were being poisoned?"

"No. I was alone. Can you do anything for me??" He was on the verge of hysteria.

I felt his forehead and placed my stethoscope on his chest, listening thoughtfully.

"We have some doctors here who most certainly can help you," I said sympathetically, taking the scope out of my ears. "I'll get you an appointment to see them in the morning."

"Oh thanks, Doc," he said, relieved. "Are you sure they'll have time to see me?"

"Oh, it shouldn't be a problem," I reassured him, putting my hand on his shoulder. "None of the doctors are going to be very busy."

I asked the nurse to get him an appointment in the Psych clinic, thanked her for the helpful advice, and went back to sleep in the lounge.

When I got back to my apartment, I fixed myself a leisurely breakfast. By nine o'clock I had finished eating and cleaning up the kitchen. I wandered around the apartment, a little disoriented. It seemed so strange that on a Monday morning I was awake, rested, and had nothing to do. I decided to go explore Hershey for the first time.

The city resembled a ghost town. The few people I saw were reporters from CBS News and the *New York Times* who were searching for people to interview.

At 8:00 p.m., I returned to the ER. The psych intern greeted me with the news that she had actually seen two patients during her twelve-hour shift.

"Ah, they're keeping you busy!" I said, smiling.

I spent the next two hours in the doctors' lounge, watching TV. I felt ridiculously, luxuriously indulgent. At 10:00, I turned off the lights and fell asleep on the couch.

I was awakened by the night nurse.

"Dr. Waymack, there's a patient here to see you."

I opened one eye. "Is he crazy?"

"No, he has a rash."

Sure enough, I found a patient with a severe rash on his abdomen. After taking a pertinent history (he'd had chickenpox as a child), I informed him that he was now suffering from shingles. I gave him a prescription for some narcotics and an appointment to the dermatology clinic for later that morning.

I returned to the doctors' lounge and slept soundly until eight o'clock, when the psych intern woke me up.

"I had a real patient last night!" I told her excitedly. "He had shingles!"

For the rest of that week in the ER, I saw between one and three patients a night, and when I left my shifts in the mornings, I was well rested and ready to explore the town, read books, and watch TV. It was without a doubt the slowest, most bizarre week an intern could experience.

By the middle of April, things had finally quieted down at Three Mile Island, and residents began returning to their homes. Patients began streaming into the ER in more routine numbers, and soon I was working nonstop through those twelve-hour shifts and getting little sleep.

It was actually reassuring to get back to my normal hectic schedule—the world hadn't suffered a catastrophe after all.

A Delightful
Whirlpool Bath

I N MAY, I LEFT THE ER and began a two-month rotation on the plastic
surgery service. I was paired with my good friend Bill Buschman, the intern
with whom I had worked for the first nine months of my internship.

On the first Friday of our rotation, Bill and I were advised that we'd be
assigned a female patient the following day. Although she was on the plastic
surgery service, the patient would be needing physical therapy. The entire
PT department would be having their spring picnic on Saturday, so they
gave Bill and me the assignment.

Neither of us had much familiarity with physical therapy, but we were
smart and capable doctors. How hard could it be?

It turned out we just needed to give the patient a bath. I mentally rolled
my eyeballs. *This is what you're stuck with when you're a lowly intern,* I thought.

The female patient had a large pressure ulcer on her hip that required
daily whirlpool baths to keep it from becoming infected. In today's medical
practice, we would surgically remove the dead tissue and skin-graft the
wound, but in 1979, medicine was not that advanced.

A physical therapist took us down to the whirlpool room and showed
us how to work it. The whirlpool was about nine feet in diameter and could
easily hold three feet of water with room to spare at the top of the sides.
There was a lift overhead, which could be rotated out beyond the whirlpool
so that a patient could be transferred from a gurney to the lift, then rotated
back and slowly lowered into the whirlpool. She taught us how to work

the lift, how to fill the whirlpool with water at just the correct temperature, and how to turn on the whirlpool jets.

It was a little insulting to have a physical therapist teach two future surgeons how to use a large bathtub. *Pretty sure we got this,* I thought impatiently.

The PT kept rambling on with unnecessary details.

"Now, once the bath is finished, you drain the tub. While the tub is draining, crank the lift up to get the patient out of the tub. Then hose her down to get the Betadine off her body. Then, rotate the lift away from the tub and dry her off."

She pointed to the far wall and said, "Over there are the towels to dry the patient, and there's the Betadine you'll need to put in the whirlpool. Put a full bottle of Betadine in the whirlpool after you've filled it with water."

I nodded impatiently. We had patients on the plastic surgery service we needed to see.

"Don't worry," said the PT. *What, do I look worried?* I thought, offended. "It's pretty simple. You shouldn't have any problems."

The next morning after we finished plastic surgery rounds, Bill and I went to the patient's room.

She was not happy to see us.

During the two weeks this woman had been hospitalized, she had endured the usual indignities hospital patients must tolerate, plus the added embarrassment of having her buttocks exposed to a team of surgeons on a daily basis. She was also taken down to the whirlpool room daily, and stripped and bathed in front of several therapists. Fortunately for her, they were mostly female, but it was still a humiliating experience. As a result, the patient was becoming increasingly depressed.

And now to top it all off, she was about to undergo a prolonged bath while two men she had never seen before watched. No, she was not happy.

We wheeled her down to the whirlpool room. Bill and I filled the tub with water, which took some time. It felt to me like the perfect bath temperature: warm, but not too hot.

While I undressed the patient, Bill went to the far side of the room and brought back a full bottle of Betadine Scrub.

"One full bottle, right?" He put it in front of my face.

I nodded.

"Yup. That's what the lady said."

Our naked patient lay on the gurney, and looked as if all desire for life had left her. She was as miserable as I've ever seen a patient.

Bill poured the bottle's contents into the whirlpool and hit the switch. We were both pleased as the whirlpool's powerful jets came on and water began vigorously bubbling up in all directions.

Yeah, I thought. *We're trainable, all right.*

Bill and I then turned our backs on the whirlpool and focused our attention on sliding the patient from the gurney onto the lift. We moved the lift around to the whirlpool, when we abruptly stopped and stared at the water. Reddish bubbles had risen to the top of the tub and were still rapidly rising. Bill looked at me with his eyebrows raised, and I responded with a hell-if-I-know sort of shrug.

I figured the patient would know.

"Is this how it usually looks?" I asked her.

The patient had a look of wonderment on her face. Her eyes were practically sparkling and she was actually somewhat sitting up on the lift, staring at the rapidly growing spectacle in the whirlpool.

"Well, sorta," she replied hesitantly.

We rotated the lift so the patient was now hanging over what had to be the world's largest bubble bath. We then slowly lowered her into the bubbles, which now extended a good two feet above the top of the tub. We lost sight of her in the mound of bubbles long before she reached the level of the water.

"Are you in the water yet?" I asked, a little concerned.

"No."

I waited a few seconds. "Are you in the water yet?

"No."

Three more seconds. "Are you in the water yet?"

"Yeah, I'm in now." We then lowered her another couple of feet.

"This can't be right!" I softly whispered to Bill.

"I know," he whispered back. "But we did exactly what the PT said!"

We began swatting the bubbles away from the general vicinity of the patient's head to ease her breathing. As the whirlpool kept roaring, the bubbles kept growing and flowing. Once they were higher than two feet above the top of the tub, they began to fall over the side. Bill and I found a mop and tried to clean them up, all the while continuing to ask the patient every thirty seconds or so, "Are you still all right?"

Each time, she said she was. Initially, the yesses had been somewhat hesitant, but as the minutes ticked by, the hesitancy disappeared and her voice increased in both amplitude and frequency.

Soon the whirlpool resembled a slow-motion volcano, as bubbles cascaded over all sides of the tub. Eventually, they reached a height of more than three feet above the tub. Although we still couldn't see our patient, well hidden in a frothy soup of red bubbles, we could tell she was fine—pleased little gasps of delight emitted from the mountain of bubbles every now and then.

"Ahhhhhhh…"

"Ohhhhh…"

"Mmmmmm…"

Finally the allotted fifteen minutes in the tub was up. We turned off the whirlpool jets, then cranked the lift with the patient out of the whirlpool. It was like seeing Aphrodite arise effortlessly from the clouds. The patient had a beatific look of supreme peace on her face.

Per our instructions, we turned on the bath hose to rinse the Betadine off. We had a slight problem with that. Even though we had cranked the lift up as high as it would go, the patient was still surrounded by an overwhelming amount of bubbles. It took at least five minutes of shooting down the bubbles with the hose before the bubble level fell enough so that we could begin to spray the patient herself.

"Ma'am, are you sure this is how things usually go?" I asked.

She hesitated. "Well, sorta," she said happily.

I got our patient dried and dressed while Bill tried to flush more of the bubbles down the whirlpool drain. I wheeled her back to her room, then returned to help Bill. It took more time to clean up than it had taken to soak our patient.

"That can't be how it usually goes," I said skeptically. Bill answered with a hell-if-I-know shrug.

The following Monday morning, as soon as Bill and I had finished rounds, we made a beeline for the physical therapy department. As soon as our whirlpool instructor saw us, she burst into laughter.

"I knew we did something stupid," Bill said, shaking his head. "What'd we do wrong??"

"You used Betadine Scrub!" she said, still laughing. "You were supposed to use Betadine Solution!"

Bill and I looked at each other blankly, then back at her.

"But you didn't tell us to use the solution," I said. "You only told us to use Betadine."

"Come on, guys," she said. "You're surgery interns. Don't you know the scrub makes bubbles?"

"Sure," I responded. *I mean, we're not idiots.* "But I never knew it would make that many!"

"Well now you do." The PT laughed, but she wasn't mocking.

"Sorry," we mumbled, hanging our heads a little.

"Sorry?!" she responded. "Do you know what you did?"

"Well, geez, we cleaned it all up!" I was a little defensive. I mean, hell, who knew giving a bath could go wrong?

"Not that," she responded, smiling. "She had been completely depressed for days. She was almost despondent—until that bath. When I gave her the whirlpool treatment yesterday, all she could talk about was the bath you gave her Saturday. You can't believe how much it lifted her spirits. She wants to know if you two can give her some more baths."

Bill and I looked at each other with a no-way-in-hell expression.

"Sorry, we're busy," I said graciously. "But we can give you the recipe for a fun bubble bath if you need it."

When my yearlong internship ended in June, I drove from Hershey to northern Virginia for my brother's wedding. The next day, I drove to Cincinnati, Ohio, to begin my surgery residency. It was a ten-hour drive through beautiful country, and I felt relaxed and free as I breathed in the warm summer air. For much of the drive, I reflected upon that strange month of April, when the ER was like a ghost town. *That month will have to rank as the most bizarre of my career*, I thought. *What an unusual coincidence that it happened during my first year of practicing medicine!*

But just as I had been wrong at the end of my first day as a third-year med student on rotations, so too was I wrong that April 1979 would be the most bizarre month of my career. During the next fifteen years, I encountered situations and events that were far more inexplicable than April had been.

My adventures were only beginning.

Part III
The Resident
1979-1983

The Wealthy Patient

MY RESIDENCY BEGAN remarkably adventure-free. I spent the first month at the Cincinnati Veterans Administration Hospital, training under probably the finest surgery resident I've ever known: Dr. Stephen Miller.

I spent the next month at Cincinnati General Hospital under a Dr. Stevenson, another excellent surgical chief resident. And again, it was a delightfully chaos-free month, full of learning and interesting cases. Not one of them involved crazy patients.

Then I rotated to the Holmes Hospital, one of the most bizarre places at which I have ever worked—and that's saying something.

The Christian R. Holmes Hospital opened in May 1929 as a private hospital where the faculty of the University of Cincinnati could send their private patients. At the time, city ordinances precluded private (paying) patients from being admitted to the Cincinnati General Hospital, which was then the only other major hospital belonging to the university.

Before medical insurance existed, you had to have a significant amount of money to afford medical care at a private hospital. In other words, the clientele of the Holmes Hospital was rich. This remained the case during my tour of duty in the late 1970s, even after medical insurance became common, and even though Holmes Hospital had been converted to an extension of the University Hospital. There was clearly a class distinction between patients at Holmes and those at the General Hospital, and it was no secret in Cincinnati.

Within the first two days of my rotation at Holmes, I noticed that a number of perfectly healthy patients were being admitted. I pulled aside a more senior resident.

"What's the deal?" I asked. "A lot of these so-called patients don't look too sick."

The resident gave a little snort and rolled his eyeballs.

"Yeah, these are the ones who are crazy rich and like to be waited on hand and foot," he said, shaking his head.

"So why don't they go to a hotel?"

He shrugged.

"Holmes is cheaper."

Now that was something I'd never seen before—choosing a hospital over a four-star hotel or a cruise.

"You wanna know something else?" the resident continued. "A lot of these patients bring their own private duty nurses!"

I was incredulous.

"But they've got plenty of nurses here!"

He shrugged again.

"Money can get you a lot of things you don't need."

One particular patient paid for a private duty nurse to sit in her room all night, while she was sleeping. After all, what was she to do if she awakened at three o'clock in the morning and wanted a glass of water? It wouldn't do to ring for one of the third-floor nurses and have to wait two whole minutes. And she certainly wasn't going to get out of bed and fetch a glass of water herself.

The pay was great for doing this "job." Not surprisingly, many nurses in their sixties or seventies—no longer interested in the hectic pace of being an ICU or floor nurse—took the job of being a private duty nurse for Holmes Hospital patients. If someone was crazy enough to pay a reasonable salary for doing nothing, why not? It was a nice piece of supplemental income to add to the Social Security checks.

As I roamed the halls of the Holmes Hospital from the 11:00 p.m. to 7:00 a.m. shift, taking care of the few really sick patients who were in the Hospital, I constantly saw private duty nurses leaning back in comfortable chairs in the corners of patient rooms. There they quietly sat, reading by a small light, while their "patients" snored away.

One night, one of these patients awakened and decided she was thirsty.

"Nurse," she instructed. "Go get me a glass of water."

The nurse, huddled over a book in the corner of the room, ignored her.

The patient was very irritated. Good grief, she wasn't paying this woman to just sit there and read!

"Nurse!" she said louder. "Get me a glass of water! Now!"

The nurse continued to stare down at her book, and blithely ignored the now irate patient.

The woman arose from her bed and stormed over to the nurse. A minute later, she thundered out of her room and marched down to the nursing station at the end of the third floor.

One of the floor nurses at the nursing station smiled at the patient.

"Hello, ma'am," she said politely. "Is there anything we can do for you?"

The woman was indignant and her lips were two thin lines.

"Yes!" she said curtly. "I am not going to pay for my private-duty nurse tonight!"

"What's the problem, ma'am?" The floor nurse was unfailingly courteous.

"My nurse *died*," the patient said, irritated.

The old nurse had indeed died while reading her book in the corner of the patient's room, and now the woman wanted to make sure she didn't have to pay for her.

On my list of appalling patients during my career, this one ranks near the top.

Eventually the dead nurse was taken to the morgue, and the surgery resident filled out a death certificate. The newly awakened, sleepy hospital administrator decided not to worry about notifying the nursing agency that had supplied the nurse until the morning. And a floor nurse got the irate patient a glass of water.

Eau de Peppermint

ON MY THIRD DAY AT HOLMES, I was working in the on-call room when I got a phone call from "Dr. Carter," one of the surgery professors at the med school.

"Dr. Waymack, I'm admitting a patient with Crohn's disease," he said. "I removed most of her small intestine a while ago, but she's having a flare-up with real bad diarrhea. When she arrives, get some routine X-rays and put her on Takadiastase."

I knew all about Crohn's—an inflammatory bowel disease—so I knew which X-rays to order. I'd never heard of Takadiastase, though.

"Yes, sir. What dose would you like to give her today?"

"Oh, the usual."

I grabbed the resident's bible—the Physician's Desk Reference, or PDR. The book lists every drug used in the U.S., along with the recommended dosage, side effects, etc. I turned to the index and looked up Takadiastase. It wasn't listed. I tried every possible spelling, but couldn't find it.

Just then, the other general surgery resident assigned to Holmes that month, Dr. Bob Linker, arrived in the on-call room. It was his night off, and he was about to leave for home.

"Hey, Bob," I said. "Would you mind stopping by the second-floor nursing station on your way out? Dr. Carter needs an order for a new patient."

"Sure. What does she need?"

"He said to put her on Takadiastase."

"Uh, what dosage?" Bob looked uncertain.

"Oh, the usual."

Bob cocked his head to one side.

"What the hell is Takadiastase?"

"Actually, I was hoping you would know."

Bob laughed and grabbed his coat.

"Well, I don't have a clue, pal. Let me know what it is in the morning."I had to make a quick decision. I could call Dr. Carter back and admit I didn't know what Takadiastase was, or I could—

In desperation, I called the hospital pharmacist, a friend of mine.

"Tim!" I said urgently. "What the hell is Takadiastase? I've got to order it for a patient!"

Tim began to laugh.

"Meet me in the cafeteria," he said. "I'll show you."

A few minutes later we sat down to dinner at a vacant table. As we ate, he pulled a Xerox copy from his pocket and handed it to me.

TAKADIASTASE RECIPE

10 grams Takadiastase granules
10 mg KCl
1 ml essence of peppermint
10 ml of water

Mix thoroughly.

I read through it, then looked up at Tim, still not understanding.

"So what the hell are Takadiastase granules?"

He shook his head.

"I'm not totally sure—it's a kind of enzyme preparation used as a starch digestant. We buy it from some company. It's not listed in the PDR, and only Dr. Carter uses it."

I looked at the recipe again.

"What's the essence of peppermint for?"

"Hell if I know. But it sure smells sweet."

"Hmm. So how much do I give?"

"You just order one dose three times a day by mouth. We send up the full recipe each time."

As soon as we finished eating, I went up to the second floor and wrote the order. The next morning, Dr. Carter arrived to make rounds. When we approached the room of his Crohn's patient, he asked, "Did you put her on Takadiastase?"

"Yes, sir! I did."

"How much?"

"Oh, the usual."

I began to wonder if Dr. Carter had forgotten the recipe for his magic potion and was hoping I would enlighten him.

We walked into the patient's room, and Dr. Carter began asking questions. The patient was now having about twenty bowel movements a day, not an unusual number for patients with severe and chronic Crohn's. Dr. Carter told her he had high hopes that the Takadiastase would fix that, and then gave her one instruction.

"Now, I want you to save the last bowel movement each night, okay?" He turned to me.

"Dr. Waymack here will inspect it first thing in the morning when he makes rounds."

The patient and I both nodded.

When you're having twenty bowel movements a day from Crohn's, what you eat tends to come out about half an hour later. Such a rapid transit time obviously precludes much digestion, so I expected to see a rather interesting bowel movement on rounds each morning. I was not disappointed.

The next day when I arrived in the patient's room, she told me that her last two bowel movements from the night before lay waiting for my inspection in the bathroom toilet. I stopped breathing through my nose as I walked into the bathroom, expecting the worst. Floating in the toilet were undigested pieces of meat loaf and mashed potatoes, along with a lot of mucus and feces.

Surprisingly, I caught a whiff of something sweet, and cautiously inhaled through my nose. Peppermint!

For the remainder of my time at the Holmes Hospital, every morning I would greet our Crohn's patient, then inspect her toilet. No matter what she had eaten, all I could smell was the wonderful sweet odor of peppermint.

A Cure for Insomnia

ONE MORNING AT HOLMES, long before sunrise, an elderly postoperative patient ("Mrs. Harris") called the floor nurse. She complained of constipation, and wanted something done about it. Immediately.

Although it was in the middle of the night, the floor nurse called the orthopedic surgery resident on call and asked him what to do.

The resident, a friend of mine, had very little patience for non-emergency phone calls in the middle of the night, and especially for a non-emergency like constipation.

"It's three o'clock in the morning," he told the nurse in an irritated tone. "This doesn't sound like a constipation problem to me, Nurse. This sounds like an insomnia problem. **Please give Mrs. Harris 60 mg of Dalmane by mouth immediately.**"

Sixty mg of Dalmane would be a hefty dose for a 200-pound, 25-year-old man. For a 100-pound octogenarian, it guaranteed twelve hours of very deep, uninterrupted sleep.

"Doctor, are you sure? That's an awful lot."

"Yes, Nurse, I'm sure."

The nurse dutifully followed the resident's orders and gave Mrs. Harris the pills.

Half an hour later, the resident—now fully awake and not happy about it—called the nurse back. He had a plan for revenge.

"Nurse, did you give Mrs. Harris the Dalmane?"

"Of course, Doctor. As soon as you told me to."

"Well, I've been thinking. If Mrs. Harris says she's constipated and wants something done about it, then we should do something about it."

"Oh good, Doctor. I agree."

"Please give her two, one-liter soap-suds enemas. And collect and measure what comes out to make sure we gave her adequate therapy."

There was silence on the other end of the line.

"Nurse?" the resident asked. "Did you get that?"

For an enema to work, the patient needs to hold the liquid inside her colon for at least a few minutes before letting go into the bedpan or toilet. With 60 mg of Dalmane on board, Mrs. Harris wouldn't even be aware she was receiving an enema, much less be able to control the timing of the release. Also, the soap suds would increase the volume and velocity of whatever came out her tailpipe.

Collecting and measuring what came out proved to be tricky, as the results of this enema ended up everywhere. And Mrs. Harris slept through the whole thing.

As some of the nurses and housekeeping personnel tried to clean up the mess resulting from the first enema, the nurse who had made the original call headed back to the phone.

"Doctor? The constipation problem is solved. The patient doesn't need a second enema!"

"Well, you never know," the resident answered. "It seemed like such an emergency when you first called me, so I think it would be best to give her the second one just in case."

When I arrived at the hospital in the morning, I started with rounds on the third floor. A foul odor on one end of the hallway made me wince, and I quickly went down to the cafeteria for some coffee.

I ran into my friend, the orthopedic surgery resident, getting some breakfast.

"Hey," I said. "Did the sewer break on the third floor? It smells awful up there!"

"Have a seat," he said, with a mischievous smile. "I'll tell you what happened last night."

The Night the
Lights Went Out

I N MY THIRD YEAR AS A SURGERY RESIDENT, I rotated at the Cincinnati VA Hospital again. One night, I was just about to close an inch-long incision in my patient's neck when all the lights suddenly went off in the OR.

I had just performed a lymphadenectomy, in which I removed a lymph node above the patient's collarbone.

A relatively simple procedure like this tended to generate a ho-hum attitude among the residents. In fact, at the end of rounds that morning, the chief surgery resident had passed the case off to me.

"Hey Waymack," he said, handing me a chart. "You won't need my help in the OR, will you?"

"Course not." This was a procedure I could do with my eyes closed.

"Excellent!" And with that, the chief headed off for breakfast.

We were all grateful for an easy day, to be honest. The day before, each of the ORs had been very busy with several major cases. In one, we performed a pneumonectomy (the removal of an entire lung); in another, a prostatectomy (the removal of the entire prostate gland). In a third OR, surgeons accomplished a portal decompression procedure in a patient with liver cirrhosis. The procedure involves bypassing the portal vein from the liver to the vena cava, the vein draining blood from the lower half of the body to the heart. It's an incredibly difficult and complex operation, as were all the others.

But a lymph node removal? Piece of cake.

The scrub nurse, circulating nurse, and a nurse anesthetist were in the OR with me. Anesthesia wasn't required for such a minor operation—for pain control, I merely injected a numbing agent similar to Novocain into the patient's neck. After we scrubbed the area with anti-microbial soap, we covered the entire patient with sterile towels, except for the small area where I would make the incision. The anesthetist was in the OR just to keep her hand under the towel covering the patient's face, so he could breathe more easily.

The operation began smoothly enough. I rapidly dissected the lymph node away from the surrounding tissues and was about to close the wound, when suddenly the room was thrust into darkness. In an instant, the OR went from brilliantly lit to pitch black. A solitary cathode ray tube emitted a faint pale green glow, displaying the patient's EKG with perhaps a tenth of a watt of light.

Although this had never happened to me before, I didn't panic. After all, the hospital had a backup generator, and I expected it would kick in within seconds. When it didn't, I still wasn't unduly unnerved, because every hospital has a backup battery, just in case the generator fails.

But the lights did not come back on, and I had a patient with an open wound. I needed to close it immediately.

None of us wanted to alarm the patient, so we were quiet. The circulating nurse blindly felt her way out of the OR to see if the power outage was localized or hospital-wide. One hallway over, the lights were working fine, and the circulating nurse found the OR head nurse on the phone with the hospital engineering office, frantically pleading for help. No one seemed to have any idea what the problem was, or how to fix it.

Meanwhile, back in the OR, the patient had become aware that our occasional subdued exchanges had ceased altogether. Fully conscious, he also detected the loss of light.

"Doc? Why is everything black?"

"Black? No no, everything's fine. You just can't see with the surgical towels on top of your face."

The nurse anesthetist promptly dropped the towels she had been holding a couple of inches above the patient's face.

Moments later, I heard the OR door open. A few seconds later, I felt someone groping my feet, then hands slowly patting up my legs and back. The circulating nurse whispered very quietly into my ear.

"Dr. Waymack, they don't know why the power went off or when it will come back on!"

For the first time since the lights went off, I was concerned. How was I to close an incision I could not see?

"Anybody got a flashlight?" I whispered.

Silence.

"Uh, sorry, Doctor," one of the nurses whispered back. We've never needed one in here. It's usually pretty bright."

"Hold on," the nurse anesthetist whispered. "I've got an idea." She blindly rustled through the anesthesia cart, lightly fingering IV tubing, needles, syringes, blood pressure cuffs, laryngoscopes, and endotracheal tubes for intubating the patients.

"Yes!" she whispered triumphantly.

A dim white light appeared in front of me—maybe a watt of power, if that, but a major improvement over the pale green glow from the EKG machine. As the light began to move towards the patient's incision, I realized what it was. The anesthetist had taken her laryngoscope and turned on the tiny bulb at the end, which is normally supposed to illuminate only the inside of the patient's airway as the endotracheal tube is being placed. This bulb provided less light than a match, but it was all I needed.

As the anesthetist held the light close to the patient's neck, I closed the incision as rapidly as possible. A few minutes later, one of the nurses wheeled the man back to the main part of the hospital, while I took off to the OR head office to find out what the hell was going on with the lights.

It turned out the entire wiring system in the fuse box had somehow melted, affecting only the portion of the hospital surrounding the ORs. Most people would've been irritated by the random bad luck—but I only felt gratitude, like I'd dodged a bullet.

Had the fuse box melted the day before, during those complicated, life-saving surgeries, we would've had a catastrophe instead of an amusing story.

An Awkward Dilemma

I N JULY 1982, I was a fourth-year senior surgery resident at the University of Cincinnati General Hospital, where one of my duties was to evaluate patients in the ER with pain in their abdomens, arms, and legs. One night, I was called down to the ER to see a patient with abdominal pain. I went directly to the nurse's station, where I found several doctors and nurses howling with laughter. The only word I caught was "erection."

In the pre-Viagra 1970s and early '80s, surgeons made a number of attempts to correct impotence, or erectile dysfunction. Probably the most successful of these had been penile implants—tubes that remained rigid at all times. Following surgery, obtaining an erection was never a problem; penile implants ensured a constant erection.

Of course, that sometimes led to embarrassing situations.

To solve this problem, medical inventors developed a new type of penile implant that remained in the "down" position most of the time; only when the patient wanted an erection did the implant assume the "up" position. The device worked as a sort of balloon, with a thin tube connecting the penile implant to a fluid reservoir located in the groin. When the patient desired an erection, he would merely pump the reservoir so that the fluid went down the tube and into the penile implant. As the implant filled with fluid, the penis became erect. When the patient no longer needed the erection, he could activate a valve implanted in the groin or in the penis by pressing against it. With the valve activated, the fluid would drain out of the penile implant and back into the reservoir in the groin, thereby ending the erection.

Or at least that's how it was supposed to work.

On this particular July evening, a man who had such an implant could not deflate his balloon, so to speak. He had successfully inflated the penile portion, and after intercourse had pressed the valve to deflate the balloon—but nothing happened. Despite repeated efforts, the rather large erection would not go down. Eventually, the man gave up and came to the University of Cincinnati Hospital where the implant had been performed. Since this was a Saturday, the urology clinic was closed, so he came to the emergency room. After some embarrassing hushed explanations to the check-in clerk, the patient was taken to one of the examining rooms.

The doctor who first saw the patient was a male third-year resident in ER medicine who was aware of penile implants and how they worked. After staring at the rather large organ, the resident told the now-uncomfortable patient that he would send in another doctor who would do what was required to make his erection go down; indeed, he described her as an expert in making erections go down.

The ER resident went looking for a certain attractive but naïve intern who had been a doctor for all of ten days. He told her that the patient in Room 11 had a problem, and instructed her to "go fix it." She nervously went into the examining room. (All interns, especially those who have been interns for only ten days, are nervous.)

While she was in the examining room, the third-year resident shared what he had just done with the other doctors and nurses at the nursing station. Their reaction coincided with my arrival into the ER, when I was trying to find the patient with abdominal pain.

As to what actually happened in Room 11, we only have the patient's side of the story, since the intern never fully recounted what had happened. Apparently, she asked the patient what exactly was the matter. Pleased to have such a beautiful woman examine him, the patient proudly pulled back the sheets to reveal his impressive organ, explaining that it was stuck in the "up" position, and he needed her to get it to the "down" position. The intern, who had never heard of penile implants, interpreted this as a most inappropriate request.

She quickly emerged from Room 11, red-faced and at a loss for words. When one of the ER crew finally regained sufficient composure to tell her about penile implants, the intern was so embarrassed she made a dash for the ladies' room, where she remained for quite some time. The ER doctors called the urologists, who eventually fixed the problem.

As for the intern, I'm not sure in which field of medicine she eventually decided to specialize, but I seriously doubt it was urology.

The Thirsty
Alcoholic

ONE OF MY PATIENTS ("Ralph") at the Cincinnati General Hospital was a chronic alcoholic. His heavy drinking led to alcoholic pancreatitis, a disease in which the pancreas, instead of secreting digestive enzymes into the intestines to help digest food, secretes the enzymes inside its own tissues. The enzymes then digest the pancreas.

Part of the treatment for this disease is a complete fast from food or drink while the patient is suffering a flare-up. This helps decrease the number of enzymes the patient's pancreas secretes into itself. Of course, fasting also makes for very hungry and thirsty patients, for even though the patients are fed intravenously, such feedings do not ease the urge to eat.

Ralph was not the most cooperative of patients, and he tended to wander the hallways in search of food or drink. Since he had no money, we didn't worry that he might go to the cafeteria or snack bar. Also, most nurses in the hospital knew Ralph, and therefore refused his pleadings for food.

At the same time, a patient on the same ward was suffering from enterocutaneous fistulas. He'd had surgery at another hospital for inflammatory bowel disease, but the operation had been unsuccessful. The patient developed a number of holes in his intestines that eventually connected to the skin on his belly, and intestinal fluid oozed out through the holes. To keep the digestive enzymes from eating the skin, bags were stuck to the skin surrounding these holes, and they would slowly fill with digestive juices. At the end of each nursing shift, the nurse would collect all the bags and measure the volume. The resident surgeon would then order intravenous fluids to replace these losses.

Although the patient was fed intravenously, the secretion of juices from his stomach, pancreas, intestines, and liver still provided for several liters of a dark green foul-smelling chunky mucus fluid to be collected each day. The loss of fluid, if not replaced, would lead to dehydration, shock, and death. When the intravenous feedings eventually improved the patient's strength, he would return to the operating room for another attempt to close the holes in his intestines.

One afternoon, this patient's nurse came into his room and emptied his drainage bags into a single container. After realizing that the container lacked volume markings, she left the container with the liter or so of green intestinal contents sitting on the cabinet, and went searching for another container.

Meanwhile, Ralph was ambling down the hall, looking for something to eat or drink. As he passed by the fistula patient's room, he noticed the container with the liter of green fluid. Without hesitation, he snuck into the room, grabbed the container, and began to gulp down the liquid as fast as he could. When the nurse returned, she was horrified to find Ralph finishing off the final drops of bilious green intestinal drainage.

The poor nurse had to page the fistula patient's doctor and explain that she couldn't measure the fistula drainage, since another patient had consumed it. The surgeon was incredulous. How did she expect him to believe such a story?

The nurse then had to explain the situation to Ralph's doctor, but he had no trouble believing her.

"Yep," he said when the nurse called him. "That sounds like something Ralph would do."

Crazy Betty

ANOTHER PATIENT OF MINE had even stranger dietary consumption habits. For years, "Betty" had lived at a state institution for the mentally challenged. She regularly tired of living there, and had learned how to get an all-expenses-paid vacation away from the institution—at Cincinnati General Hospital.

Like the state penitentiary prisoners, Betty swallowed inedible objects. Spoons, glass thermometers, random objects—anything within reach was fair game. The head nurse would then call an ambulance to transfer Betty over to the Cincinnati General Hospital. These episodes happened once every few months, and Betty became as well known at our hospital as she was at the state institution.

Naturally, the staff at the state institution became very careful about not leaving spoons or thermometers around for Betty to eat. Inevitably, however, a new nurse would arrive on Betty's ward and would forget or disregard the warnings.

Betty's arrival in the ER became routine and predictable.

"Welcome back, Betty!" would be followed by an X-ray, after which we would admit her to the ward and wait for the object to pass in a bowel movement. This was the end result about ninety percent of the time, but occasionally the object was too large to pass from her stomach into her intestines. At that point, we would open up Betty's stomach, retrieve the object, then close the incisions. We called the operation "exploratory celiotomy," or "laparotomy," or "gastrostomy," all of which describe the removal of a foreign object from the body.

Probably a quarter of the surgical residents during their career at the

Cincinnati General Hospital had performed at least one such operation on Betty. This all changed in the early 1980s, when endoscopy became widely used. A surgeon would insert an endoscope, a long flexible tube with a light at the end, through Betty's mouth into her stomach. The surgeon would grab the swallowed object with a pair of forceps, and would then pull the endoscope along with the object out through Betty's mouth.

The first time this endoscopic procedure was used on Betty, the surgeon paid to have the spoon mounted on a wooden plaque with the inscription, "This spoon was removed from Betty Smith's stomach with an endoscope by Dr. John Smith on April 16, 1982." He hung the plaque on the wall of the endoscopy suite at the hospital. A few months later, a second plaque commemorated another doctor's successful procedure.

One day before endoscopy became commonplace, Betty swallowed a thermometer. The medical student who presented the case to a visiting local surgeon happened to have memorized the list of every inedible object Betty had ever swallowed, and recited it in full.

The visiting surgeon, out of perhaps both incredulity and curiosity, visited Betty's room. She was sitting on the bedpan, having a bowel movement. The moment the surgeon entered her room, Betty got off the bedpan, and proudly showed it to her new guest: a bowel movement that contained a thermometer.

The surgeon thought for sure the team was playing a trick on him—until Betty, right in front of him, reached down into the bedpan, picked out the thermometer and, without wiping it off, swallowed it again. Apparently, she wasn't quite ready to go back to the state institution.

Another time, Betty tried to fly. A new but experienced nurse had arrived on her ward at the state institution, and she did not take any guff from patients. When Betty ate a spoon from her breakfast tray, the nurse merely told her to not flush the toilet when it came out in her bowel movement. The nurse was concerned that the spoon might block the pipes.

For the rest of the morning, Betty tried to make the nurse understand that eating a spoon is supposed to guarantee an immediate trip to the hospital. The old battle-axe, however, wasn't buying it.

Betty thus decided to go to the hospital on her own. She crawled out her window and started heading in the general direction of the Cincinnati General Hospital. Eventually, she stopped on the side of a tall embankment next to an intersection with a stoplight. When a convertible drove up to the light and stopped, Betty saw her chance and took it. She jumped from the side of the embankment, down onto the trunk of the convertible, then slid into the passenger seat.

The driver was understandably startled at the sight of a woman flying down into his passenger seat. He never even got a chance to regain his composure, because within a couple of seconds of landing, Betty grabbed the cigarette lighter and swallowed it.

Her trick worked. As soon as the light turned green, the driver sped toward the Cincinnati General Hospital. When he pulled up to the emergency entrance, a nurse from the ER was already waiting.

"Hi Betty!" she said, helping her out of the car. "Nice to have you back."

I don't know if the driver ever got his cigarette lighter back, but it's probably just as well. The empty hole in his car will always remind him of a great story to tell passengers.

The Mysterious
Gunshot Wound

I N MY FINAL YEAR OF RESIDENCY, I was surgery chief resident at
Cincinnati General Hospital. One evening, I was in the ER X-ray department examining the films of a patient's leg when the junior surgery
resident walked in, seeking advice. He began by recounting the symptoms
of a middle-aged woman with vague abdominal pains, then reported her
past medical history, which included an appendectomy.

This history eliminated appendicitis from my list of diagnoses (appendicitis is one of the four most likely causes of severe abdominal pain), but
also increased the likelihood that a bowel obstruction was causing the pain
(bowel obstruction is one of the four most likely causes of severe abdominal
pain in someone who has had a prior operation).

As the junior resident and I discussed the potential diagnoses that fit
this patient's symptoms and signs, the technician handed us the abdominal
X-rays she had just taken of the patient we were discussing. The films were
unremarkable except for one thing: the patient's entire abdomen was filled
with unmistakable images of buckshot.

I looked at the resident, aghast.

"She's been shot?!" I asked incredulously. This new bit of information
greatly increased the likelihood that the patient had a bowel obstruction
resulting from adhesions from the operation I assumed she'd had to repair
the gunshot wound.

The resident looked as surprised as I did.

"Shot?" he responded, puzzled. He peered at the films. "Well, yes, it does look like she's been shot. But she didn't mention it!"

I couldn't believe he'd been so careless in a physical examination.

"Uh, didn't the incision from the operation clue you in?" I asked, irritated. "Or did you forget to examine the patient thoroughly?"

Again the resident stammered and looked thoroughly confused.

"Well, uh…"

I put down the films, and impatiently took the resident with me to the exam room. A pleasant, middle-aged woman was lying on the examining table, covered by a gown and a sheet. After introducing myself, I began taking a history—thoroughly this time—and asked the patient many questions. Eventually I got around to asking her about prior surgeries. She said that the only one she'd ever had was an appendectomy.

"But what about when you were shot?" I asked.

She gave me a confused look.

"What?" she answered, her eyebrows raised. "I've never been shot."

Uh-huh, I thought.

Several times, I'd actually had patients deny that they'd been shot, even after I'd pointed out the scar left by the bullet exit hole, or even after seeing the X-ray that showed the bullet still inside their body. Presented with this seemingly incontrovertible evidence, these patients would still look me right in the eye and swear they had no idea how or when the bullet wound or the bullet got there. Some claimed the X-ray was "lying."

So when this woman refused to admit she'd been shot, I simply asked her to pull up her gown so I could examine her. She had an old appendectomy scar on her abdomen, but no other scars or wounds.

Hmm, I thought. *She must've been shot in the back.*

I rolled the woman over and looked for wounds in her back. There were none. By this point, I was dumbfounded, and the junior resident and I searched her body for the entry wounds we knew had to be there. We even checked the inside of her vagina, just in case someone had stuck a shotgun up there. No wounds, anywhere. Completely perplexed, we next examined her name bracelet to make sure the correct name was on the X-ray. It was.

I decided to go in another direction for the time being. Since bowel obstructions eventually prevent you from being able to eat, I asked when she had last eaten.

"Dinner last night."

"And how much did you eat?" I asked. "A lot or a little?"

"Oh, quite a bit," she responded happily. "I had three squirrels, a couple of potatoes, some bread—."

My head snapped up. "Squirrels? Where did you buy them?"

She looked at me as if I'd lost my mind. "You can't buy squirrel meat, Doc! My husband shot them for me."

"With buckshot?"

"Actually, yes. Why?"

I patted her hand and told her she'd be just fine. (Buckshot passes out intact with a bowel movement, just like raisins swallowed by a toddler.) Moments later, I left the room along with the junior resident and, once outside, apologized to him.

As for the patient, she merely had a mild case of indigestion. Either she didn't chew her food very well, or she didn't bother to spit out the buckshot pellets.

Another Day, Another Stab Wound

URING MY YEAR AS CHIEF RESIDENT, I seemed to attract an inordinate number of cases with stab wounds to the heart. Stab wounds are always cause for concern, but a heart puncture is the most dramatic of emergencies. If you can fix the wounds within a few minutes of the stabbing, the patient will do well and the operation will be both quick and easy. On the other hand, if you delay treatment, the patient will die.

One week when I was on call, I operated on patients with stab wounds to the heart two nights in a row. The next night, I fell into bed exhausted, hoping to get a couple of hours of sleep. Around one o'clock, my beeper went off with a "4571 stat" call. I hightailed it down to the ER.

Rushing in, I found nurses and residents working urgently to stabilize a very large, muscular man. His feet hung over the wheeled stretcher, and I quickly sized him up at about 6'6", 240 pounds. A one-inch puncture wound next to his left nipple looked innocuous, but the patient's jugular veins were distended, and his blood pressure was dangerously weak.

The fourth-year resident briskly gave me all the patient's stats and his diagnosis.

"It's not a tension pneumothorax," he said. "His lungs are up on X-ray."

"Get him to the OR," I barked. "Now!"

We swiftly wheeled him to the OR, arriving just as the man's blood pressure disappeared completely. I didn't wash my hands or the patient's skin, nor did I put on a sterile gown or sterile surgical gloves.

"Ten blade!" I barked to the scrub nurse. She immediately handed it to me. I pushed hard and cut all the way down to the bone in one stroke.

"Sternal saw!"

The scrub nurse anticipated each of my orders, and passed each instrument as efficiently as a relay runner passing a baton.

I split open the patient's chest, then briskly took Metzenbaum scissors from the nurse and opened his pericardial sac. I had been working on him for less than a minute.

The stab wound had caused blood to leak out from inside the heart into the pericardium, the sac in which the heart is enclosed. Now it was filling with blood, squeezing the superior and inferior vena cava vessels and preventing them from carrying blood to the heart, like a kink in a hose. The patient was in a state of pericardial tamponade; his blood pressure plummeted to zero because he had no blood left in his heart. He was now clinically dead.

As soon as I snipped the pericardial sac with the scissors, I relieved the external pressure, thus allowing blood to flow freely into the heart. I reached into his chest with one hand and gave the heart a couple of gentle squeezes, until it began to beat on its own.

Unfortunately, as it started pumping, blood began gushing from the stab wound in the heart's side. I instantly pressed my index finger against the hole, plugging the hemorrhage. The bleeding stopped, at least temporarily.

During the frantic sixty seconds it took me to open the patient's chest, the anesthesiology resident was also desperately working to save the patient's life. She had just as much to do as I did, if not more. During that minute, she managed to place an endotracheal breathing tube through the patient's mouth down into his lungs. She started an IV line in his arm and poured in fluids, then hooked the endotracheal tube to the breathing machine and set the machine on 100 percent oxygen—a smart thing to do when someone is in shock.

Now that the immediate danger had passed, I could close the incision in the patient's heart. I stood with my finger plugging the hole in the patient's heart and finally allowed myself to exhale.

Another one saved, I thought, relieved. At the same time, I marveled at how routine these penetrating heart wounds were becoming. Three nights on call in a row, I had saved patients with nearly fatal stab wounds.

As I relaxed, the anesthesiology resident continued to perform intricate tasks in rapid succession. Once the patient's blood pressure returned, she turned back the rate at which the IV fluids were infusing. She took his blood pressure and pulse rate, and hurriedly sent off blood samples to the lab. She grabbed the OR anesthesia record forms, which required a report on the patient every five minutes during surgery, and usually required several minutes of attention prior to starting the operation. Finally, she was about to place the patient's arms on the arm boards attached to the OR table, and secure them with tape—again, something you would normally do before an operation.

I turned my head and saw the senior surgery resident, the medical student, and the nurses working together to return the OR to its usual level of absolute sterility. The resident and med student were just outside the room, vigorously scrubbing their hands at the sink. The scrub nurse and circulating nurse inside the OR were separating the sterile instruments from those I had contaminated. The circulating nurse grabbed a bottle of liquid antiseptic soap to pour onto the patient's chest.

I then turned back to make sure the anesthesiology resident had turned back the rate of infusion of the intravenous fluids.

Suddenly, hands grabbed the back of my head and yanked it down toward the patient's open chest. My eyes were only inches away from the exposed heart when I vigorously pulled myself backward, yanking my finger from the hole in the patient's heart. Blood gushed out the side of the heart like a firehose. I struggled to stick my finger back in while cradling the heart in my other hand, all the while fighting against whoever was trying to shove my face into the patient's open chest cavity.

"SHIT!" the anesthesiologist exclaimed. "I forgot to put him to sleep!"

While she had been scrambling to readjust the rate of infusion of the intravenous fluids, set the ventilator dials, start keeping the required anesthesia record, and the other eight or nine critical things she needed to do simultaneously, the patient's cerebral blood flow had resumed. His brain was again being perfused with oxygen-carrying blood, which thus revived his brain from a state of death. The patient awoke to excruciating pain in his chest, and did what any half-conscious person would reflexively do in such a situation: grab the body part that feels like it's on fire.

Unfortunately for me, my head was between his hands and the pain.

The resident and med student, having finished scrubbing their hands and arms, walked into the OR to see a huge patient in a wrestling match with me on the operating table, the patient's chest wide open and blood squirting out of his heart.

The med student's eyes opened wide as tennis balls.

"What's going on?" she exclaimed, horrified.

The senior resident didn't miss a beat in responding.

"Oh, it's fine," he said calmly. "Dr. Waymack likes his patients to be actively involved in their own care."

While I continued to struggle with the patient—blood intermittently spewing out of the hole in his heart whenever he managed to knock my hand from his heart—the anesthesiology resident worked feverishly. She filled a syringe with pentobarbital and injected it into the patient's vein. About a minute later, the patient stopped struggling and went to sleep.

With my finger finally plugging the hole uninterrupted, I turned my head to the scrub nurse.

"4-0 Prolene, please," I said evenly.

I helped the senior resident suture the hole. Five days later, the patient was sent home.

Thankfully, he never remembered what had happened in the OR. There's a saying we surgeons have: "If not anesthesia, then amnesia." In other words, if you fail to put the patient to sleep, just make sure he doesn't remember your mistake.

As for the anesthesiology resident, I don't blame her for what happened. She had far too many things to do in very few seconds to be blamed for failing to do one. In the greater scheme of things, putting a clinically dead patient to sleep was pretty low on the priority list. The critical task, which she did, was to keep the patient alive.

A Perfect Record

O N MY LAST DAY as surgery chief resident, my team was on call from 9:00 a.m. Saturday to 9:00 a.m. Sunday. After that, my residency would be over. Since Saturday was the busiest trauma day of the week, and June was one of the busiest trauma months, I assumed my residency would end with a bang: a dozen critical cases would surely arrive in the ER and be admitted to my surgery team.

I was counting on it.

During the preceding four years and eleven months as a resident, I had been on call for ER admissions on more than 600 days. On each of those days, I had always admitted at least one patient to my department. Every single day."

This unbroken streak began to assume increasing importance to me as my chief resident year began to draw to a close. I had always figured I would never achieve perfection in anything—but I did have a rare perfect record of admitting patients when my team was on call.

As I drove in to work that final Saturday, I was relaxed and happy. It was a sunny June morning, the air smelled fresh and clean, birds were chirping, and soon I would be treating bullet wounds or stabs to the heart. I couldn't wait. During rounds that morning with my team, I was positively giddy.

"Dr. Waymack, how many do you think we'll get today?" a med student asked hopefully.

"At least seven," I predicted confidently. "Four of them will be trauma."

After morning rounds ended, I took a nostalgic tour of the hospital. I wandered from the surgical area to the ICU, from the ER to the OR, remembering the endless adventures I had experienced there during the previous four years at Cincinnati General Hospital. I thought about how much of my life I had left behind in those corridors. I thought of how many lives I had saved. I remembered the triumphs and the tragedies. And I waited to be paged to the ER for the first admission of this hot June day.

Surprisingly, nothing traumatic had arrived in the ER by noon. No gun shots, no stab wounds, no car wrecks; not even an appendicitis. By 4:00 p.m., I was impatiently skulking around the ER, demanding to know where the patients with surgical problems were being hidden.

At six o'clock, my team and I had dinner in the hospital cafeteria. The mood was solemn, but I was philosophical.

"God's saving up all those patients for us," I said, taking a bite of meat-loaf. "We're going to get *flooded* with them tonight. Just wait."

The med student and two junior residents nodded glumly, chewing their food in silence. They knew how important this was to me.

I took a big gulp of coffee, wiped off my mouth, and stood up.

"Come on, boys," I said, trying to look cheerful. "We'll get some trauma cases soon. Keep your chins up!"

With that, I went off to my on-call room to grab a few minutes of sleep, which I knew would be interrupted as soon as patients started arriving.

I awakened with a start at midnight, and grabbed my beeper. No, it wasn't a 4571 (ER) call, just the resident in the next on-call room, snoring loudly. I got up and went down to the ER to search for my patients. None had come in.

Where the HELL was everyone?

I called my senior resident, Dr. Paul Glen, who in less than twelve hours would be the new chief resident replacing me.

"Paul!" I exclaimed, desperate. "I need an admission—any admission! I want my perfect record intact, dammit!"

He talked me off the ledge, and assured me he'd find someone to admit.

Around two in the morning, I wandered through the ER one last time as a resident, anxiously looking for a patient to admit. In resignation, I trudged back up to my on-call room for a little bit of shut-eye.

The next thing I knew, the sun was shining in my room. My watch read

6:15. I sighed and got up. I couldn't believe that on the final day of my residency, after 600 days of being on-call in the ER, I would lose my perfect record.

There's no way an admission will come in between 6:15 and 9:00 on a Sunday morning, I thought dolefully.

In all my five years as a resident, I could not remember a single surgery patient coming in at that time of day on a Sunday. People who shoot each other are in bed at that hour, the drunks are sleeping it off, and most everyone else is on their way to church, too slowly to cause traffic accidents. And if you've awakened with a bellyache on a Sunday morning, you usually wait a couple of hours for the pain to pass before you decide to come into the ER with full-blown appendicitis.

A few minutes past seven, I met Dr. Glen in the cafeteria for breakfast. He said he was sorry, but there was absolutely no one who needed to be admitted. In fact, the ER had been almost empty the whole night. I finally realized how absurd it was to be begging for an emergency trauma, and laughed it off as a bizarre ending to a bizarre five years as a surgical resident. We started talking about his upcoming year as chief resident, and my upcoming year as a research fellow.

Rounds were supposed to begin that morning at 8:00, so I headed back to my on-call room to shower, shave, and put on fresh clothes. At 7:45, as I stepped out of the shower, my beeper went off: 4571. I dialed the number, and Dr. Glen answered, jubilant.

"Waymack! You won't believe this. A trauma patient just arrived and the next surgery team doesn't start taking admissions for another hour, so he's yours!"

"Great!" I exclaimed, thrilled. "What's he got?"

"He's been stabbed in his left arm and it bagged his brachial artery. He's totally pulseless below the elbow. We'll have to repair it. Do you want an angiogram?"

"Nah—don't waste the time and money. We know where his artery was cut."

"Sounds good. I'll call you when we reach the OR—they can take us right away."

"Great. Hey—how'd he get stabbed?"

Dr. Glen laughed. "He found out his girlfriend was having an affair, so they got into a big fight. He told her he wouldn't tolerate any infidelity shit, so she stabbed him."

"Okay," I said, chuckling. "Call when you reach the OR. I'll make rounds with the rest of the team."

A few minutes later, we began rounds and returned to our usual talkative selves. We rounded on the patients in the ICU on the second floor of the hospital, then moved on to the general surgery ward on the fifth floor. When my final rounds as a surgery resident ended an hour later, I still had not heard from Dr. Glen. Puzzled, I paged him.

"Hey! How come we aren't in the OR yet? It's been over an hour since you called me!"

"Well, we have a slight problem," he explained. "The patient won't sign the OR consent."

The guy was nuts. If he didn't have the artery fixed, he could lose his arm.

"He says he won't sign the consent until he talks to his wife and gets her approval."

I exhaled in exasperation.

"Fine. OK, I guess. But why does he need his wife's—"

It took me a second.

"What?" I exclaimed into the phone. "His *wife?* He has a wife? I thought it was his girlfriend who was having the affair!"

"Yeah," Dr. Glen agreed. "Crazy, right?"

It seemed a fitting conclusion to a very challenging yet unbelievably rewarding five years.

Eventually, the cheating husband did get his wife's permission to operate, and by noon Sunday, his arm was fixed and I was on my way home. As I walked out of the hospital, I seemed to float to my car in the parking lot. It felt better than walking out after your last final in college, or finishing the MCAT. I felt an overwhelming sense of pride—not just in myself, but in my profession, too. Perhaps that feeling is unimaginable to those who haven't spent five years working more than 100 hours a week, fighting death and the ravages of disease.

As I drove home that day, it occurred to me that my buoyancy might be due to another reason. For the first time during my residency, I was well rested after a Saturday night on call for trauma. For once I was wide awake, fully aware of the scenery. I stared at the bright sun I had seen so little of for the past seven years, and contemplated how different the next few years as a research fellow would be. Among other benefits, there would be no more nights on call in the hospital, at least for a long while. I would be sleeping in my own bed at night again. I would see the sun when I drove into work each morning—no longer would I be blearily driving to the hospital long before dawn.

From this day forward, I thought, *my life will resume a more normal and sane existence. No more craziness.*

No more craziness? Wrong again.

Part IV
The Researcher
1983-1987

The
Sacrificial Pig

A FTER FOUR YEARS OF COLLEGE, four more of medical school, and five years as a surgery resident, I was finally qualified to announce to the world that I was a surgeon. Instead of joining a practice, however, I chose to spend the next four years in a research lab, working toward a Doctor of Science (Sc.D.) degree.

It took more than a few sleepless nights to make this decision—after all, I knew I would have to make a considerable financial sacrifice to pursue a scientific career. My fellow surgeons would be making a truckload of money while I worked in a lab for more limited pay. Still, I had to go with my heart. I wanted to contribute to the field of medical research and become a faculty member of a university surgery department—not fix gall bladders and hernias. (Not that there's anything wrong with doing that!)

I began with a study of immune dysfunction in burn and trauma patients. Because such patients suffer from a temporary damage to their immune system—putting them at great risk of developing infections—medical researchers were trying to enhance immune function to supranormal levels.

Immunology is also an issue with transplant surgery, but here the problem lies in the opposite direction. Transplant researchers were trying to *suppress* the immune system, which automatically tries to reject a transplanted organ. I was so fascinated by this work in immunology that I completed a clinical fellowship in transplant surgery while I worked on my Doctor of Science degree.

Being a research fellow wasn't always exciting, but it certainly had its advantages. For the previous five years in residency, plus the two years before that in med school, I'd had an extraordinarily challenging schedule: every other night on call, thirty-six-hour shifts, and up every morning by five on the days I actually got to sleep in my own apartment (instead of working through the night in the hospital). During my years as a researcher, I got to go home every night and get seven luxurious hours of sleep. I didn't have to be at the lab until 8:00 a.m. Best of all, I didn't have to deal with drunken patients who cursed me, or drug addicts who threatened me when I refused to give them prescriptions for narcotics.

Another plus were the stories I heard from my fellow surgical researchers, which—even by *my* standards after seven years of crazy experiences—sounded too wildly improbable to be true.

I shouldn't have been surprised when other surgeons corroborated their accuracy.

Charlie Baxter was possibly the greatest burn surgeon ever. I met him when I attended the American Burn Association's annual meeting as a fifth-year surgery resident, and we eventually became close friends. A born storyteller from Texas, Charlie was as gifted at spinning a tall tale as he was at operating, so naturally I was skeptical when he started telling me about a pig who got burned.

I wasn't the only curious one. We were sitting at a table in the hotel bar—Charlie, me, and a handful of other burn surgeons. Charlie's reputation guaranteed that he'd always have an audience when he began telling stories, and on this night he'd had our full attention for over an hour.

"Then there was the pig story," he began, downing a shot of whiskey and wiping his mouth. Charlie had a thick raspy twang that sounded like sand paper rubbing on concrete, and the effect was alternately unnerving and mesmerizing.

"About 1965 or so, this doctor in New England said he'd come up with

a magic cure for burns," Charlie said. The long, drawn-out way he pronounced "New England" made it clear that he didn't think too highly of
the so-called doctors up there. "He had an ointment that made the burns
'simply dissolve away,' he said. He called me and some other burn surgeons
to tell us of his wonderful discovery, then said he'd bring the magic cream
to the burn meeting in Florida. He was going to burn a pig, apply the
cream to the burned pig, and show how it magically cured the animal!"

Charlie and the other surgeons roared with laughter, slapping the table
and hooting. I thought it was funny, but not for a second did I believe any
of this actually happened. Magic ointment on a burned pig? I may have
been just a few years out of med school, but I'd never heard of any doctor
that stupid. Apparently, the other surgeons had.

Charlie continued once the howling subsided.

"Well, that there Nooo Eeeengland doctor went out and bought himself
a real live mini-pig—you know, the kind that's about the size of a beagle—
plus two first-class seats on Eastern Airlines to Florida. The day before the
meeting, this guy fills one suitcase with his clothes and the other with his
magic ointment, some surgical equipment, and some sodium phenobarbital to put the pig to sleep. And, of course, he packs the iron he's going to
burn the pig with."

Some of us winced, imagining the poor creature.

"The next morning, this guy drives to the airport in Augusta, Maine, to
catch the first leg of his flight to Atlanta," Charlie said. "When he gets up
to the check-in counter with his mini-pig on a leash, the ticket agent says,
'Sorry, sir, but that pig is not getting on the plane. Yes, sir, I realize you have
two first-class tickets, but we don't allow pigs to fly with the passengers.'"

Charlie took another sip of whiskey and continued.

"Well, that there Nooo Eeeengland doctor didn't give up, no sir. He
takes the two suitcases and pig into the men's room, empties all his clothes
from one of the suitcases, and dumps them into the wastebasket. Then he
takes out the phenobarbital and injects the poor little pig. While Piglet is
conking out, that nut takes out one of the surgical knives and pokes air
holes in the empty suitcase, then puts the pig in there! He takes the two

suitcases back to a different ticket agent and checks just the one with his equipment, then carries on the bag with the pig." (In the 1960s, carry-on luggage wasn't X-rayed.)

Charlie leaned forward and paused for dramatic effect.

"There was, of course, a problem. When the good doctor got off the plane in Atlanta and took his carry-on bag to the men's room to give the pig a drink of water, what he found when he opened it was a very dead mini-pig. He dumps poor Piglet into the wastebasket, then catches his connecting flight to Florida."

Charlie shook his head in disbelief.

I've often wondered about the reaction of the men who saw the dead pig in the restroom wastebasket. Even for someone with Plutonium Medallion status as a frequent flyer, that had to have been an unprecedented event. What about the janitor who emptied the garbage? The poor guy must've had nightmares for weeks.

"At this point, the story starts to get really bizarre," Charlie said, without a hint of irony. "Ya see, this doctor was not one to be discouraged. He continued on to Florida without his pig but with his magic cream. And when he arrived, he called all the nearby grocery stores and tried to buy a live mini-pig. Sadly for him, none of them stocked live mini-pigs; they only sold parts of dead, regular-sized pigs."

Other bar patrons started to congregate around the bar within hearing distance of Charlie's raspy voice.

"That evening, this doctor sat in his hotel room discouraged, but not defeated," he continued. "Here he was, at the burn meeting, with no burn to treat. So he did what any crazy doctor would do—as God is my witness, he really did! This guy takes off his pants, plugs in the iron, lets it get nice and hot, then lays it on his thigh."

There was a collective *ooooooooh* from the group, and most of us winced and reflexively covered a thigh.

"How he withstood the pain, I have no idea," Charlie said, shaking his head. "But he left it on his thigh until he had a third-degree burn in the shape of an iron."

This was just too much for a couple of the junior surgeons; their credulity had been stretched just a little too far.

"Oh, come *on!*" one of them exclaimed, with a look that said *You gotta be kidding me.* The senior burn surgeons all chuckled and nodded that yes, it was true. I still had my doubts.

Charlie smiled and took a few puffs from his cigarette.

"Awww, you haven't even heard the best part yet!" he exclaimed, enjoying the attention. "The next morning, that Nooo Eeeengland doctor went down to the meeting. He found me and a few of the others, and told us to come up to his room to see the burn cream in action. 'How'd you get the pig into the hotel?' I asked him. He explained that the pig was dead and in a wastebasket in a men's room in the Atlanta airport, so he had burned himself instead."

Charlie started laughing so hard he ended up in a coughing fit. He took a drink of whiskey.

"Well folks, there ain't no way anyone's going to refuse that invitation," he said. "So after breakfast, I go up to this nut's room with Curtis Artz, John Moncrief, and Basil Pruitt." These three surgeons, incidentally, were part of the group that founded the American Burn Association.

"We get inside, close the door, and this guy drops his pants!" Charlie did a good impersonation of a man shocked by something horrific. "Lo and behold, there's a fresh third-degree burn in the shape of an iron on his thigh! Damnedest thing I ever saw! And while everyone's staring at it, the guy applies his magic cream and places a bandage around it. 'Come back in a few hours!' he says. 'You'll see it really works!'"

This was the part everyone had been waiting for.

"At lunch time, we go back up to the guy's hotel room," Charlie recounts. "The good doctor drops his pants, removes the bandage, takes a tongue blade, and scrapes away the magic cream and the entire burn wound."

Charlie grabbed a butter knife to illustrate on his own thigh.

"It turns out," he explained, "that this 'magic cream' contained nothing but a lot of enzymes that ate away the dead skin. This was how it had worked on the pigs up in Maine. There were, of course, two problems.

First, what was left after the burn had been removed was not a healed wound, but a raw one. Second—as you fellas know—pigs are able to constrict most any blood vessels in such wounds, and this keeps them from bleeding excessively. But ya know, Doc, we humans can't!"

Another collective *ooooooh* as the surgeons knew what happened next.

"That nut starts bleeding like Niagara Falls," Charlie said, making gushing noises and using his hands to illustrate blood spurting. "As soon as the tongue blade wipes away the dead tissue, blood starts flying everywhere. Everyone's racing around the room looking for something to stop the damn hemorrhage."

The bartender, who'd been leaning over the counter listening to the story, guffawed.

"And you say this guy was a *doctor?*" he exclaimed. "Where the hell did he get his medical license?"

Charlie let out a bellowing laugh. "Aww, probably somewhere in Nooo Eeeengland!"

Someone impatiently urged Charlie to finish the story.

"Well, finally someone wraps the wound with towels from the bathroom," he continued. "Then someone calls down to the drug reps who had exhibits at the meeting, and they send up dressings, ointments, and surgical tape to the room. And for the rest of the meeting, every morning and evening someone had to go up to this nut's room and change his dressing."

One of the junior surgeons asked the question that had been on everyone's minds: "Why the hell did he do something so stupid?"

Charlie chuckled.

"We asked him," he said. "All he could think to say was, 'Well, at the time it seemed like a good idea.'"

Gunfight in the Pig Lab

A NOTHER STORY I HEARD BEFORE I started my research came from Dr. Wes Alexander, one of the early pioneers in transplantation and the doctor who ran the lab where I trained. Dr. Alexander not only did transplants in patients, he also practiced his techniques by transplanting organs in animals. Today, such research primarily uses mice and rats, but back then, transplant surgeons frequently used pigs.

One day, Dr. Alexander ordered a large number of young piglets to do a series of experiments. There was an even number of the small animals, since one piglet would be the donor and one the recipient. However, one of them died before the experiments started, so the leftover piglet was transferred to a separate section of the hospital, where a veterinarian and his staff cared for all the animals awaiting research experiments. Hundreds of small creatures, including rats and mice, were humanely caged and fed in separate rooms. Once all the pig experiments were completed, the research fellows didn't go to the pig rooms anymore—and they promptly forgot about the poor little creature.

Over the next six months, the veterinarian's staff took care of the pig. Initially, the piglet was small and pleasant, but eventually it became a full-grown hog, with the reported personality of a wild boar. Eventually, the staff complained to the veterinarian, who then called Dr. Alexander on the phone.

"Uh, Doc?" he asked. "When do you plan on conducting your experiment with this hog we've been boarding? He's become quite unpleasant."

For a few seconds, there was silence on the other end.

"I'm sorry—what hog?" Dr. Alexander asked, perplexed.

"You remember the cute piglet you sent over a few months ago? It's now a large hog. Actually, we think it might be a boar."

"Oh, yeah. Um, let me get back to you on that."

Dr. Alexander called all the research fellows and found that, no, there was no plan for the hog. After some brainstorming, he came up with one. He called the vet back.

"Hey, could you hold the hog until the weekend?" Dr. Alexander asked.

That Saturday, Dr. Alexander and two research fellows backed a pickup truck to the loading dock of the hospital. Meanwhile, other research fellows were preparing a large pit for a pig roast. The three men cautiously entered the pig lab, and Dr. Alexander aimed a .22-caliber revolver at the large hog, who was not at all pleased to see him. He pulled the trigger before the hog could charge.

Upon being shot, the hog went from unpleasant to very angry. Grunting ferociously, it charged Dr. Alexander, who dove out of the way just in time—onto a pile of porcine fecal material. The other two men scrambled madly to avoid being trampled, and they also slipped and fell onto the floor, which was now covered with pig poop and blood from the hog's bullet wound.

Dr. Alexander quickly got up onto his knees and fired off another round from the revolver. The bullet was a clear hit, but again the gunshot merely seemed to further anger the hog without slowing it down. Blood and poop continued to fly about the lab in a mad melee as the gunfight continued. The revolver was nearly empty before the hog finally collapsed and died.

The three men also collapsed onto the floor, thoroughly covered with blood, sweat, and dung. To make matters worse, they knew the gunshots had been loud enough to attract a lot of attention. The hospital police would surely be there any minute.

"This was not a good idea," Dr. Alexander admitted, chagrined. "We've broken a lot of hospital rules. Pretty sure some city and state laws, too."

They sat in silence for a few seconds.

"I know a good lawyer," one of the guys said helpfully.

The men cleaned themselves up as best they could while awaiting their arrest. Then they waited and waited. Finally, Dr. Alexander had an idea.

"Why don't we just get the hell out of here while we can?"

They quickly left the lab, dragging the pig carcass and dumping it into the back of the pickup truck. They raced to the waiting barbecue, and were happy to see that no police followed them. They did wonder about that, but they weren't about to ask any questions.

The absence of the police remained a mystery for about a year, until a seemingly unrelated incident shed some light on the policemen's failure to chase the pig posse.

A patient died on the clinical transplant service, and his family did not take the news well. One of the brothers screamed at the surgery resident and chased him with a knife, yelling that he was going to kill that son of a bitch who murdered his brother. The resident ran down the hallway at breakneck speed and locked himself in a closet. A nurse called hospital security.

"There's a crazy man waving a knife and threatening to kill a resident!!" she shouted into the phone.

The hospital policeman was apparently unimpressed.

"What the hell do you want *us* to do?" he said.

"Come save the resident's life!" the nurse shrieked. "That's your JOB!"

"No way," said the policeman. "Call 911!"

Given that insight into the hospital security's lack of interest in securing the hospital, it made sense why they never investigated the gunfight in the pig lab. Actually, I'm surprised the guards didn't just take off in the opposite direction once they heard the shots.

The Day the AC Went Out

ALTHOUGH I GOT MY SECOND DOCTORAL DEGREE at the University of Cincinnati, I did my research training at the Shriners Burn Institute, an old four-story building just down the block from the University of Cincinnati Medical School. Two floors of the building were dedicated to patient care, one to administrative functions, and one to research.

I spent most of my time on the research floor. It was a very productive time for me, and I published over forty scientific papers in four years—a feat I couldn't have accomplished but for my exceptional research team. My mentor, Dr. Wes Alexander; a couple of excellent technicians, Phil Miskel and Sara Gonce; and a very proficient secretary, Vicki Greene, were tremendous assets. I was also fortunate to have Ron Greenlee as an unofficial member of my team, who was invaluable on several occasions—and never received proper credit.

Ron worked in the hospital maintenance department and had no degree or title; to be honest, I don't know if he even finished high school. But he had outstanding common sense and a remarkable problem-solving ability, both of which always came in handy in the research lab.

One blistering, steamy July day in Cincinnati, some college-trained idiot in the Shriners administration with no common sense decided to have the air conditioning undergo routine servicing. Naturally, this required shutting down the air conditioning for the day. Why the administration didn't schedule the servicing in, say, April was a mystery to all of us.

The research floor had no windows, and the only windows in the entire building—on the patient floor—did not open. Not surprisingly, by ten o'clock the temperature inside the building began rapidly climbing past 90°F.

My first concern was not my own comfort, but how my research rats were going to survive in the heat. Some of them had undergone heart transplants. Others had been burned, all for the cause of science and helping human burn victims. The rats had been treated with drugs for weeks. I had invested six weeks of hard work on these rats, and if they died from the heat, that time would have been a complete waste.

While I was agonizing and trying to come up with a solution, Ron approached me.

"Dr. Waymack, this heat's gonna kill all your rats," he said, concerned. "Why have they turned off the air conditioning?"

I couldn't answer him.

Ron and I stood in the windowless animal room and stared at the endless racks of animal cages hanging above the tile floor. To facilitate easy cleaning with a water hose, the entire room except the ceiling was tiled, and the floor sloped down to a drain in the corner of the room. Unfortunately, the tile also held in the heat, and my rats were beginning to pant. I figured that by noon my animals would all be dead, and those six weeks of hard work would go down the drain.

Ron had a thoughtful look on his face as he surveyed the room.

"Don't worry, Doc," he said reassuringly. "I'll take care of it." He left the room, leaving me heartsick with my heat-stricken rats.

I went back to the chemistry lab room, dejected, and began drinking a Coke. I wiped the sweat off my face and mentally composed a sternly worded letter to the Shriners administration.

About an hour later, my technician Phil came briskly into the lab.

"Paul!" He beckoned for me to follow him. "Come on. You've got to see this."

I gamely tagged along behind Phil, who headed straight for the animal room. I knew I was going to find a hundred dead rats when we walked in.

As I entered the animal room, the temperature felt like a breezy 72°F. I was startled to see that the rat cages, normally centered around the middle of the room, were pushed up against the far wall. In the center of the room was a huge pile of ice, about four feet high and six feet in diameter. Immediately in front of the pile of ice, an enormous electric fan was blowing the cold air that came off the pile of ice toward the cages.

Ron Greenlee stood by the pile of ice with a shovel in his hands, looking quite pleased.

"We're buying all the ice from every 7-11 in the area," he explained.

Throughout the rest of the day, as the ice melted and drained along the sloped floor, Ron shoveled fresh ice onto the pile. The only comfortable room in the entire hospital was the animal room, and all my rats were just fine.

I know I said it many times, Ron, but thanks again for keeping my rats from a sure death, for helping the cause of science to advance, and for saving six weeks' worth of work. You rescued every rat in that room, and I will always be grateful for your initiative and quick thinking.

Fred the
Magic Rat

FRED WAS A RAT, but not just any rat. Of all the rats in all the experiments I performed, Fred led by far the most memorable life. He was born in a rat-breeding farm in Maine that sold animals to science labs at a hefty price—Fred cost ten bucks in 1984, so about $25 today. The reason for the high price is the pedigree; these rats are under stricter breeding control than most regulated canine breeders anywhere in the world.

Fred was genetically as close as possible to being a twin of all the other white Lewis rats I bought from that farm. This genetic similarity helped the research considerably, for if I gave a drug to fifty rats and a sugar pill to another fifty, I knew that any difference in their response was due to the drug. The farm shipped Fred and forty of his nearly identical siblings to me when they were eight weeks old.

At that time, I was performing experiments to learn how to keep patients from rejecting their transplants. I would transfer blood from a Fisher rat to a Lewis rat and administer various drugs for one to two weeks, then transplant a Fisher rat heart into a Lewis rat. I would hook up the heart to the blood vessels inside the rat's belly, and every day I would pick up the Lewis rat and feel its belly to see if the heart was still beating. On the day the beating inevitably stopped, I would record in my lab notebook that the heart had been rejected. My research led to a better understanding of how drugs and blood can affect the immune system, and I wrote a number of articles on the subject of organ rejection in transplant patients.

Most of the rats rejected their transplanted hearts after a week, if they had received no fresh blood. If they had received a blood transfusion, the rejection was delayed to two weeks; with a transfusion along with certain drugs, rejection didn't occur for up to three weeks. Fred, however, never rejected his new heart. It just kept beating through four, five, and then six weeks. Eventually, the weeks turned into months. I was astounded.

Finally, eager to write up my results, I got my notebook. Next to Fred's identification number, in the column that listed the number of days until each heart was rejected, I wrote: >90 days.

In the months I had been examining Fred (at the time known as Treatment Group B, Animal #11), I had grown rather fond of him. He was quite friendly, had a cute way of wiggling his whiskers, and never attempted to bite me (a favorite activity of his species). I was very reluctant to sacrifice the little guy, but the experiment was over, and I knew I needed to make room for a new rat due to arrive from the farm. I stared sadly at Fred, trying to get up the nerve to give him the required lethal dose of pentobarbital. I decided to wait until after I had finished my shift at the pediatric burn clinic.

I didn't have any official responsibility at the clinic; this was supposed to be a period of pure research for me. For a while, though, the Shriners Burn Institute was short of staff surgeons, and they asked me to staff their pediatric burn clinic on Tuesday afternoons. Since they were allowing me to work in their labs, I figured it was the least I could do for them.

A pediatric burn clinic is an awful place if you don't like hearing children scream. Even young children have memories, and their recollections of when they were patients in the burn hospital are primarily those of great pain. All the children I saw ranged from frightened to terrified when they returned to the hospital clinic for a follow-up visit, even though they never experienced any pain during those visits. I liked helping the kids, but dreaded the crying and screaming.

While I stood there forlornly watching Fred happily skitter around his cage, with no clue what awful fate awaited him, I suddenly had a brilliant idea. I reached into the cage and gently coaxed Fred into my hand. I tucked him in the large pocket on the front of my white doctor's jacket, then headed off to the clinic. Fred seemed quite comfortable, and soon was quietly napping.

My first two appointments were with teenagers whose burns had healed quite nicely. Fred continued to nap in my pocket. My third patient was a three-year-old boy who began to cry uncontrollably as soon as I entered the room. I smiled warmly at him and said hello, but he just screamed loudly and hung on to his mother for dear life.

That woke Fred up.

I reached into my pocket and pulled the little guy out. The crying stopped immediately. I handed Fred to the boy, whose face suddenly transformed from terror-stricken to wide eyes and a look of awe. For the next five minutes as I examined the boy—feeling his scars, checking the motion available in his joints, and making a notation of all these examinations—the boy played with Fred, completely unaware of my presence.

The boy's mother stared at the animal, then me, then the nurse. She was clearly delighted that her son had calmed down, but she had a slight look of concern.

"Is that a rat?" she said cautiously.

"Oh, don't worry," I responded. "That's just Fred." On the spur of the moment, I had given Animal #11 a name.

As soon as I finished the examination, the boy reluctantly gave Fred back to me. I returned him to my pocket, and the nurse and I walked to the next patient room. As soon as the boy and his mother were out of earshot, the nurse grabbed my arm.

"Dr. Waymack!" she whispered sternly. "You can't bring a rat to clinic!"

I smiled reassuringly.

"What do you mean I can't? I already have! And would you rather have the children screaming?" I raised my eyebrows at her.

She couldn't fight my logic, and from that day forward, Fred accompanied me to every clinic.

Eventually, the clinic personnel adopted Fred. When Halloween arrived, a few of the nurses even made him a costume. He became a beloved mascot, and I could tell Fred loved the attention. I suspect another reason he enjoyed going to the clinic was because the staff gave him a piece of candy at the end of each shift, and candy tastes a hell of a lot better than Purina Rat Chow.

Fred continued to calm screaming children for many months. It almost seemed like magic: I would enter a room to find a screaming child, hand Fred over, and the screaming would immediately stop.

Only once did Fred fail to calm a terrified child. The nurse and I entered a room to find a small girl howling and crying, while her mother kept trying to sooth her. I took Fred out of my coat pocket and handed him to the screaming little girl. Instantly the room became silent as she took the friendly rat into her tiny hands. About half a second later the room once more filled with ear-piercing shrieks, far louder than the girl's screams had been.

The terrified mother jumped up and ran from the room.

"IT'S A RAT!!" she shrieked hysterically.

Needless to say, this caused quite a commotion in the waiting room. The end result was that the clinic administrator gently suggested that perhaps Fred should be retired from clinic duty. Happily, the head nurse in the clinic had become so taken with Fred that she took him home as a pet for her son.

Fred spent almost a year in pampered retirement before dying and going to rat heaven. During his short but meaningful life, Fred advanced the cause of transplant medicine by showing how a certain drug along with a blood transfusion could decrease the risk of transplant rejection. He brought comfort to frightened little patients and simultaneously soothed the clinic staff's rattled nerves. Finally, the sweet little rat brought great pleasure to the clinic nurse's son.

If doing good for mankind qualifies a rat for heaven, then yes, Fred definitely deserved to go there. He most assuredly did a lot of good for his human friends—more so than many humans.

All for Science

FRED WASN'T THE ONLY RAT I cared about, of course—I worried about each and every one of my animals. The data I generated from each of their results would help to advance the cause of medicine, plus I had put in an enormous amount of effort, hard work, and time into each rat. These little guys were my babies.

One day, I was alone in the animal operating room, doing rat heart transplants. The six rats that were to receive the hearts had already undergone two weeks of hard work. I had given them blood transfusions, followed by twice-daily drug injections until the day of surgery. I had put in long hours during the weekdays with my little rats, and had even come in to the hospital twice a day on two consecutive weekends.

The heart transplants went quite smoothly. I gave each Lewis rat a shot of pentobarbital to put it to sleep (in the animal lab, I was anesthetist, nurse, and surgeon). I next removed the hearts from the donor rats and transplanted them into the recipients.

By early afternoon, I had finished all six transplants. Five had gone well, and the recipients were now back in their cages awake and skittering around. The sixth rat, however, had not yet awakened. I nervously kept an eye on him, and was devastated when he eventually stopped breathing. Apparently, the combination of anesthesia and surgery had been too much for him.

My despair at the rat's apparent demise wasn't just from compassion as a co-sentient being—I was panicked that I might lose a rat in which I had invested so much hard work. Instinctively, I cupped it in my hands and did what any doctor does when a patient isn't breathing: mouth-to-mouth resuscitation. To be totally accurate, it was more like mouth-to-face resuscitation, since my mouth was bigger than the rat's entire head.

I was hard at work trying to resuscitate my rat when our research dietitian from Thailand, Orrawin Trocki, walked into the animal OR. The first thing she saw was my mouth pressed up against the rat's face, in what must have looked like a passionate embrace. She immediately backed out of the room, and hurried down the hallway.

I was so focused on the rat that I never saw the dietitian enter the OR. I did, however, hear her alarmed voice in the hallway.

"Dr. Waymack kissa the rat!" Orrawin exclaimed, horrified, to someone in the hall.

At that point I happily saw that the sick rat was now breathing on its own, so I gently placed it back on the table. I went to the OR sink and began washing out the rat hairs that now coated the inside of my lips and mouth. This is actually more challenging than it sounds—those little hairs stick to the inside of your mouth like they've got suction cups on them.

While I was washing my mouth out, a few curious colleagues carefully ventured into the OR to see if the story was an exaggeration.

"Did you really just kiss a rat?!" my research tech Sara Gonce asked, laughing.

I pretended shock and indignation.

"What? I never heard such a ridiculous story! Where'd you hear that?"

As for the rat, he survived. The experiment was saved, and I could add one more crazy story to my growing list.

Pistachio Nuts
and Fish Oil

THE AVERAGE PERSON doesn't give much thought to what researchers feed rats. They eat anything, right? Scraps of food, Purina Rat Chow, perhaps? No sir, not with our rats. Ours were specially fed, and a lot of thought went into their diet.

One day I stopped by the office of Dr. Bill Chance, one of the world's foremost researchers in the field of nutrition and brain function. He was forever trying various dietary supplements in rat experiments, and the day I stopped by to see him, the newest supplement had just arrived. They came in a barrel, and Bill had just taken the top off and was staring down at the green pellets.

"What's that?" I asked.

"Oh, a new rat food formula," he responded. "It's high in arginine. I want to see if it alters hypothalamic function in my rats."

I studied the green pellets carefully, picking one up and smelling it. I wrinkled my nose.

"How do you get them to try new food?" I asked. "Are you sure they'll eat this?"

"Oh sure!" he answered confidently. "My rats have never turned anything down."

He paused for a moment.

"Well, come to think of it, maybe it's because I don't offer them any alternative," he continued. "You know, like how parents get their kids to eat vegetables? You eat it or you go hungry!"

Recalling my own stubborn refusal to eat certain vegetables even in the face of starvation, I wasn't convinced.

"Suppose they hate the taste? Will they still eat it?" I asked.

Bill shook his head. "I honestly don't know. They've eaten everything I've ever given them."

Like any scientist, I was curious. Since there were no rats nearby to test out Bill's claim, I took one of the green pellets and ate it myself. The taste was a sickly combination of pistachio nuts and pure sugar, and I felt a little nauseous chewing and swallowing it. But since Fred the Rat had liked candy so much, I figured the other rats would probably love it.

I was interested to see if other humans would like it. Dr. Alexander's two secretaries each had a notorious sweet tooth, so I grabbed a handful of the pellets and headed down the hallway to their desks.

"You won't believe this new candy I bought!" I exclaimed, handing each of them a piece. "It's too sweet for me, but what do you think?"

They popped the pellets into their mouths and chewed for a few seconds, thoughtfully calibrating the taste.

"You're right," said one. "This is too sweet even for me. Where did you get it?"

"Oh, it's the new stuff Dr. Chance is trying out for the rats," I said.

They both made sour faces at me.

"Ewwwww! Dr. Waymack!"

They ran to the water fountain and rinsed out their mouths.

"Gee," I said, wondering what the big deal was. "It's not like I fed you a rat!"

We tested the next experimental rat food in the animal lab. It was made with fish oil, which at the time was all the rage in the scientific community—it was reportedly good for everything from cancer therapy to heart disease prevention. Unfortunately, it stunk to an unimaginable degree.

Dr. Alexander thought perhaps the fish oil might be good for burn patients, so he devised a plan to surgically insert feeding tubes into the stomachs of guinea pigs. Next, the animals would be burned over a third of their body. (That sounds horrific, I know, but remember this was research that would save the lives of human burn victims.) Half the guinea pigs would receive a standard diet through their feeding tubes, while the other half would receive a diet with a very high concentration of fish oil. Two weeks later, the animals would receive a lethal dose of pentobarbital and be autopsied.

I was not usually involved in Dr. Alexander's nutrition projects. But he asked me to assist Orrawin, the research dietitian, with the medical aspects of the experiment. She had been a little wary of me since the rat-kissing encounter, but she agreed to work with me since no one else was available.

We surgically inserted feeding tubes into the stomachs of forty guinea pigs. For the next three weeks, Orrawin took care of everything: she nursed the animals following their operations, burned them, fed them the prescribed diets for two weeks, then put them to sleep. At that point, she turned the guinea pigs over to me for the autopsies.

I hadn't seen (or smelled) the animals since the day I put the feeding tubes into their stomachs, so I was overwhelmed by their stench. Unsurprisingly, after being pumped full of fish oil for two weeks, the guinea pigs now reeked of dead fish. I began the first autopsy by removing the skin, and was overcome with nausea. In med school, I thought the formaldehyde smell of cadavers would be the worst odor I'd ever encounter in my life. I was wrong.

For the next four hours I worked in the animal OR, performing autopsies of dead guinea pigs that smelled like rotten week-old fish. I knew that if I survived that day, I could survive anything.

I had almost completed the final autopsy when a tour came into the animal OR. Since Shriners Burn Institute is a world-renowned hospital, teams of doctors and scientists from all over routinely came to visit. On this day, a group from Japan was making rounds. As I stood hunched over the animal OR table completing yet another guinea pig autopsy, five Japanese surgeons walked in with their tour guide.

The guide told them about all the cutting-edge research we were doing at Shriners, and explained that I had been doing experiments on burned guinea pigs. While she was going on about how remarkable and ground-breaking this research was, the Japanese surgeons' attention was clearly elsewhere. I saw five pairs of eyes scanning the room suspiciously. They looked at my dead guinea pigs with a slightly confused look. As the tour guide continued speaking—apparently ignoring the strong smell out of professional courtesy—the visiting surgeons tried nonchalantly to walk around the lab, sniffing subtly. I'm sure they must have thought there were dozens of dead fish lying somewhere in the lab, but they didn't stay long enough to find out. Eventually the guide finished her talk, corralled the wandering visitors, and headed them off to the next room in the building.

Whenever I smell fish now, I think of those confused Japanese surgeons. What explanation did they finally come up with to explain the awful stench? The odd experience must have led to some interesting conversations that evening back at their hotel. Whatever story they landed on, I'd be willing to bet they never ordered fish for the remainder of their visit to the U.S.

The Frozen Rats

THE JAPANESE SURGEONS were not the only visitors who wondered about the culinary consumption at the Shriners Burn Institute. One incident began when I was in Europe, giving a lecture on my research. While I was gone, my research tech Phil Miskell checked on my rats every day. Whenever one died, he put a sticker around its leg with the date, placed it in a plastic bag, and stored the bag inside the lab freezer.

I had been gone nearly a week when I returned early one morning to find eight rats in the freezer. I placed the plastic bags on top of my lab bench to thaw so I could autopsy them.

The rats were still hard as a rock a couple of hours later, thanks to the -100°F temperature in the lab freezer. At the rate they were thawing, it would probably be many more hours before I could autopsy them.

I put the rats in a large paper bag and took them up to the clinic floor where there was a small dining room with a snack bar and microwave. I was the only one there. I placed four rats onto a large paper plate and set them in the microwave for a long defrost cycle.

After several minutes, I removed the now-thawed rats and put them back into the paper bag, then microwaved the other four rats. While these rats were defrosting, I turned around and found to my surprise that the room was no longer empty. A family of four was looking at me in shock and horror, and I realized they had just seen me remove several rats from the microwave and replace them with another group.

I was briefly at a loss for words. Should I offer a lengthy explanation on the importance of science? Maybe assure them the rats were germ-free and on a paper plate? Perhaps say nothing and quickly retreat? I decided to go with a little levity.

"They're great with ketchup!" I said enthusiastically.

The family hurriedly left the dining room. I'm sure they'll be telling that story for years whenever they play "Two Truths and a Lie."

The Sino-American Burn Conference

ALTHOUGH THE PAY for a career in academic medicine is far less than what one could make in private practice, academics does offer a few unique advantages. One of these is the ability to interact with physicians from all over the world. Along with the benefits of such exchanges, however, come obvious challenges.

In 1985, during my research fellowship at the Cincinnati Shriners Burn Institute, I attended the first Sino-American Burn Conference in China. It was a time of awakening and change for the communist country. Mao Zedong had been dead for about a decade, and his death had been followed by a titanic power struggle. Deng Xiaoping, a moderate who years earlier had tried to change Mao's policies, took over the reins of power in 1978. Mao's widow and three other Chinese politicians—the so-called "Gang of Four"—were imprisoned and later tried in 1980–81 for their activities in the Cultural Revolution.

By the early 1980s, Deng was espousing an interesting philosophy, at least from a communist perspective. True to his statement in 1961, "it doesn't matter whether a cat is black or white; if it catches mice it is a good cat," Deng announced an ambitious plan of opening the economy to capitalism—so long as it improved the quality of life.

As part of this plan, Deng began to open up China in a way it had not seen since before World War II, and one of the results was a series of international scientific, medical, and business conferences held throughout China. The meetings were ostensibly to teach Chinese scholars, doctors, and scientists about Western methods and knowledge, but an ulterior motive was to show the rest of the world that Red China offered the potential for great rewards from the investment of capital and ideas.

One of these efforts to improve relations between China and the Western world was the Sino-American Burn Conference, at which I was asked to give a lecture and moderate one session. The conference was held in Chongqing, because China's premiere burn surgeon, Dr. Li, lived there. Now a bustling, sophisticated metropolis with more than 30 million people, Chongqing in 1985 was quite a different city. Unlike the coastal cities of Beijing and Shanghai, Chongqing is far inland—a thousand miles west of Hong Kong—and was largely unfamiliar with Westerners in the '80s. In fact, the burn conference was the city's first experience hosting an international event.

From Cincinnati, I flew to San Francisco, then on to Hong Kong. The flight, with a refueling stop in Honolulu, took about sixteen hours. After a night in Hong Kong, my colleague Ed Robb and I joined a dozen Western burn specialists on a small, aging Russian aircraft (circa 1960) that Air China had bought second-hand. The flight was supposed to take three hours, but because it was raining in Chongqing, the pilot decided to go to Chengdu instead, since it was the nearest airport where the weather was clear. Chengdu sits on a large plain in the Sichuan Basin about 250 miles west of Chongqing, and the two cities are separated by the Longquan mountain range.

Within half a minute of landing, police ordered us off the plane; we learned later that no one from the control tower had notified them that the plane had been diverted from Chongqing. We also learned that no plane from a Western country had landed in Chengdu since about WWII—and Hong Kong, as a British territory, qualified as "Western."

I'm 6'5" and don't find airplanes particularly comfortable, so I was the first one off the plane. I walked down the stairs and strode briskly across the tarmac and into the terminal. A dozen smarter (or luckier) Western burn specialists followed a good distance behind me.

Several grim-faced men in military uniforms—the national police, as it turned out—greeted me. One of them barked something in Chinese and stretched out one hand impatiently. I assumed he wanted my passport, so I handed it to him. He flipped through the pages and then glared at me. He said something to the other policemen and they all began questioning me in heated, rapid-fire Chinese. They gestured at my passport and several shook their fingers at me angrily.

Nervously, I looked back toward my so-called friends, who were taking an awfully long time to enter the terminal. I needed a translator like a drowning man needs air. I shrugged helplessly as the police continued to demand answers from me.

The pilot finally entered the terminal and explained the situation to the guards. The problem, he explained to us in English, was that all our visas were for Chongqing, not Chengdu, and the Chinese were real sticklers for having the proper papers—especially if you're not Chinese. The police stopped barking at me and returned my passport. Though they didn't smile, they did bow politely. I quickly returned their bow and started looking for the rest of my group, anxious to park myself at the back of the line for the remainder of the trip.

The adventure didn't end there. Since all flights from Chengdu to Chongqing were grounded, we quickly ran to a nearby train station and hopped on. Only after the train left the station did we realize that none of us had a timetable for train arrivals, nor could we read the signs in the stations. Still, we were fairly confident that at least one of us would recognize "Chongqing" on the loudspeaker once we got there.

The fifteen-hour ride was an adventure. A bullet train today will make the journey in about two hours, but in 1985, the railway took a languorous, circuitous route over the Longquan mountain range, through forests and gorges and on to the Yangtze River Valley. My good-natured colleagues were excellent company, and although no food or water was available on the train, we did have a couple of containers of Scotch.

We arrived in Chongqing by nine the next morning, and an English-speaking Chinese doctor welcomed us and put us on a bus to the hotel. I could write many dozens of pages on the typical oddities and humorous misadventures that any traveler might encounter in a foreign land, but it's not too difficult to imagine what might happen when a 6'5" Caucasian in plaid wool slacks meanders around a remote city that hadn't seen many Westerners since before World War II.

The Sino-American Burn Conference, in contrast, was rather typical of most medical meetings I had attended throughout the world. Our Chinese hosts attempted to mimic the Western-style medical meeting in its design, with its endless series of speakers who give presentations on some medical topic. Such lectures are normally followed by multiple questions from the audience. These questions are usually sincere efforts to seek clarification on some point.

The first morning of the burn conference, one American burn specialist spoke on the use of antibiotics in burn patients. The presentation was followed by half a dozen questions, all from other Americans. Next up was another American who gave a talk on the use of nutritional support in burn patients, which was followed by another half-dozen questions, all from Americans. The third speaker was Chinese, and he gave a presentation on the use of antibiotics in Chinese burn units. This was followed by another half-dozen questions, all from Americans.

As this scenario kept repeating itself the first day, we Americans began quietly asking each other why we were the only ones asking questions. At the same time, it turned out, the Chinese were asking each other why the Americans were so rudely asking questions after such fine presentations. Their reaction makes sense if you remember that in the early 1980s, one did not ask questions in China. Such an action might indicate you disagreed with the speaker, who might be more powerful within the Chinese Communist Party than you. Even a respectful "disagreement" could be hazardous to one's career, if not one's health.

At the end of the first day's meetings, there was a quick cultural powwow with some of the Americans and Chinese who already knew each other.

After the Chinese politely asked what was going on with all the questions, we explained that it was not meant as a sign of disrespect, but rather of scientific curiosity. Or, as I told one of my Chinese friends, we were so intrigued with what they had said during their talks that we wanted to learn even more.

To our great pleasure, the next morning at the end of the first talk, some of the Chinese doctors gingerly raised their hands to ask questions. Progress!

Four years later, sadly, asking questions and expressing grievances did result in a certain incident in Tiananmen Square. But as the Chinese philosopher Lao wrote, "A journey of a thousand miles begins with a single step."

After the meetings, our Chinese hosts took us on a few field trips in Chongqing. The first was to a burn unit in a local hospital. As I toured the unit, I saw patients whose burns covered much of their bodies. For patients with such severe burns, it's essential to get their joints moving, or else the joints will stiffen and become permanently useless.

Unfortunately, even the simple act of bending a pinky finger can cause horrific pain in these burn victims. In the U.S., burn surgeons send physical and occupational therapists into patients' rooms to make them bend their fingers, wrists, knees, and every other joint. If the patients can't or won't bend them, the therapist must do it for them. Such actions usually result in great screams of pain by the patient. But it has to be done. Otherwise, even if you save the patient's life, he will merely end up crippled and incapacitated for the rest of his life.

As I watched the Chinese patients, I was astonished to see that not only were they doing painful bending exercises without screaming, but also without the assistance of a therapist. I leaned down to one of the English-speaking Chinese doctors.

"How do they do it?" I asked, amazed.

He looked a little puzzled, as though he didn't understand the question.

"They do it because we tell them it is necessary and they *have* to do it," he said matter-of-factly.

My next surprise came in the operating room. I was observing Chinese surgeons perform an excision and grafting procedure, in which they cut away the dead (burned) skin from the patient and replaced it with thin pieces of healthy skin from unburned parts of the patient's body. This "donor skin" is thin enough so that the spot from which it is removed will heal in about ten days. The operation is simple if a surgeon has enough donor skin to cover the entire burn, but often the donor skin is inadequate.

One of the ways to solve this problem is by "meshing" the skin. This technique involves running the healthy donor skin through a meshing machine designed by Dr. James Carlton Tanner, Jr. in 1964. The machine makes a series of small parallel cuts in the skin, allowing it to be serrated and stretched over the burn area. After the graft first heals vertically into the wound, it next heals horizontally to close the holes.

If the skin has been cut so that the holes are very large, you need to have something to cover the holes while you wait for the horizontal healing, or else the wound will desiccate or become infected. In the U.S., we place cadaver skin on top of the meshed skin graft. Once the holes in the meshed skin have healed, the cadaver skin falls off on its own.

In the 1980s, the Chinese did not have a meshing machine, but they were aware of the technique. Resourcefully, they came up with a Chinese variation of the procedure: technicians cut donor skin grafts from the burn patient into postage-stamp-size pieces, then cut similarly sized holes into strips of cadaver skin and sewed the patients' pieces of skin onto the cadaver-skin holes. The whole process was tremendously labor-intensive, requiring hundreds of holes and pieces.

I watched in amazement as a dozen technicians sat on sterile back tables in the OR working on this new patchwork-quilt skin, while surgeons and nurses meticulously removed the burn wound tissue from a patient. Once the new skin was ready, the surgeons sewed it onto the newly excised burn wounds.

The efficiency and hard work of the teams was awe-inspiring, but not a bit surprising; the disciplined work ethic of these Chinese was unlike any I'd ever seen. Three decades later, the stunning economic prominence they've achieved is no shocker to anyone who's seen Chinese workers in action.

Our next field trip was to a liver disease ward. In 1985, viral hepatitis and cirrhosis in China were almost inescapable, since both illnesses stemmed from a commonplace occurrence: the ingestion of contaminated food or water. Most cases of cirrhosis—liver malfunction due to long-term damage—weren't due to alcoholism, but to the aftermath of the body's healing process in response to viral hepatitis. Scar tissue begins to replace normal liver tissue after sustained damage, and eventually shuts down all liver function.

Even worse, the damage to the liver caused by the scarring means that blood is unable to flow properly. The increased pressure causes esophageal varices: veins in the esophagus that become distended and can eventually burst, causing massive internal bleeding. Although surgery could stop the bleeding, these operations tend to cause liver failure, so physicians instead use blood transfusions and other nonsurgical methods.

In the liver disease ward, I saw a number of patients who were obviously bleeding from esophageal varices. Physicians were treating them with standard Western-care techniques, such as a Blakemore tube: a medical device inserted orally that inflates a gastric balloon into the stomach, and a separate esophageal balloon to reduce blood flow. The patients were also receiving blood transfusions. In the U.S., blood goes directly from the donor into a sterile plastic bag, then from the bag into the recipient. A small amount of the blood is stored separately for testing, so the bag never needs to be opened (and thus contaminated).

In China, they ran the same tests we did, but the way they administered the blood was very different. Each patient receiving a blood transfusion was hooked up to an old-fashioned glass intravenous bottle hanging upside down by the bed. A tube ran from the bottom of the bottle into the patient's vein, just like they did in U.S. hospitals.

As I observed one patient receiving a transfusion, what caught my attention was not the narrow neck of the bottle where the tube exited, but the other end of the bottle. The flat bottom, now flipped around on top, had been cut away, and a thin piece of cheesecloth—the kind used to strain yogurt—covered the open bottle. I stared at this contraption for a few seconds, trying to figure out how they got blood into the bottle before the bottle was turned upside down to hang beside the patient's bed.

A nurse came by just then, holding a large flask of blood. She checked the hanging bottle by the patient's bed, noted that it was nearly empty, and started refilling it with blood from the flask. She checked the other patients' bottles, topping off each one with blood from the flask, much like going down a row of plants with a watering can.

How do they test for cross-matching? I wondered in disbelief. *What if the blood type isn't compatible with the patient?*

Another nurse must have seen the puzzled look on my face. The cheese-cloth, she explained, was to keep flies from getting into the blood. After a week of surprises in China, that was an explanation that made perfect sense.

The Worst Flu
of My Life

MY RESEARCH WASN'T LIMITED to just animals, of course. After I'd identified promising treatments using rats or pigs, I needed to test them out on human volunteers and diseased patients in clinical trials. One such trial took place when I was an associate professor of surgery at the University of Texas Medical Branch on Galveston Island. My colleagues and I wanted to see whether prostaglandin E caused trauma-induced immunosuppression.

Prostaglandin E is a hormone-like substance the body makes in response to a number of situations, including trauma. Burn trauma suppresses the body's immune system, predisposing the patient to potentially lethal infections, and we wanted to investigate whether that immunosuppression resulted from the flooding of prostaglandin E into the bloodstream.

We took white blood cells from healthy volunteers and put them into cell cultures. We mixed prostaglandin E with half the cells in an *in vitro* test and added nothing to the other half. We found that in the prostaglandin E culture, the white blood cells stopped working; in the other culture, the white blood cells continued to work normally. We thus reached the conclusion that prostaglandin E caused the trauma-induced immunosuppression.

The next obvious step to prove our hypothesis would have been to inject animals with prostaglandin E and see if it impaired their immune function. However, the obstacle to doing that kind of *in vivo* test (performed inside the body), is that prostaglandin E is broken down within a couple of minutes of entering the body. We had to wait until a few years later, when a drug company manufactured a prostaglandin E analog that lasted for several hours after being injected inside the body.

I was the first burn surgeon to obtain this compound and inject it into rats. As with the *in vitro* test, I separated the rats into two groups and gave one group the hormone analog and the other a placebo. I exposed both groups to bacteria, fully expecting the rats that had received the prostaglandin E analog to die at a far greater rate than did the group that had received the placebo. To my astonishment, the opposite happened: the rats that had received the analog had twice the survival rate of those who received the saline placebo injection.

I was so convinced this couldn't be correct that I repeated the experiment two additional times. On both occasions, I got the same results: the analog improved survival. When I published these findings, they were initially greeted with some degree of skepticism. Gradually, however, the doubters acknowledged the validity of my experiments.

I wondered, though, if perhaps the rat was different from a human, immunologically speaking. Perhaps prostaglandin E stimulated a rat's immune system, but suppressed a human's. Of course, this time I had to use real people to test my theory. After obtaining permission from the appropriate government regulatory agencies, I rounded up nine healthy scientist-volunteers… and me. That's not exactly standard protocol, but I was curious to see the effects, and I didn't want my colleagues to have all the fun.

The plan was to test our immune function by running blood tests before and after taking the prostaglandin E for a week. Everything started out normally on Monday morning. The ten of us had our blood drawn, and then we began taking our analog pills four times a day.

I had no side effects that first day, but my eight colleagues certainly did. They quickly developed diarrhea; one of them later confided that he'd had twelve bowel movements that day. Another volunteer, a professor, disclosed that he'd (unintentionally) had a bowel movement while sitting at his desk. We already knew that prostaglandin E could stimulate bowel function; we just didn't realize the magnitude of the effect.

Normal volunteers probably wouldn't have continued taking the pills after that first day. These eight volunteers, however, were researchers, and they were committed to science. They knew the experiment was important, and bathrooms had plenty of toilet paper. Frankly, I thought they were all exaggerating, because I was feeling just fine.

The second day of the experiment was a typical summer day on Galveston Island. The temperature was in the high 80s, and the humidity was characteristically oppressive. As I headed to work that morning, though, it curiously felt like a cold front had blown in. I took my pills and began some paper work. An hour later, I felt as if I had the worst case of the flu in my life. My head was pounding, all my muscles were aching, and I was having shaking chills. I assumed I had caught the flu, and considered withdrawing from the study. After all, this was supposed to be a study on how prostaglandin E affects a normal immune system, not a compromised one.

At lunchtime, I weakly made my way to the hospital cafeteria for some soup. Another of the scientist-volunteers was doing the same thing, and he looked worse than I did. Suspicious, I tracked down the other volunteers and found out they each felt like it was the worst case of the flu they'd ever had. We agreed we would continue taking the nasty pills because the experiment was so important—but only until Friday morning.

The next three days were unusual. Despite the steamy tropical weather, I shivered uncontrollably. While everyone else on the island was wearing shorts and tank tops, I wore heavy sweaters and thick wool pants. Naturally, I attracted a lot of attention.

Also, I noticed my symptoms peaked and ebbed, depending on how long it had been since the last dose. I felt the worst within minutes of taking a pill. But since my kidneys were constantly flushing the drug out, the prostaglandin E level would gradually fall so that I no longer felt as if I were about to die, and that blissful feeling would occur right before the scheduled time for the next pill. The up-and-down cycle was agonizing.

That Friday morning we all took our final dose of the prostaglandin E analog. An hour later, we had blood drawn. When the results came back, the data showed that our immune systems were running at approximately

150 percent of normal. Eventually, after many more experiments, we made the startling discovery that the prostaglandin E did in fact stimulate immune function, much in the same way that the flu stimulates immune function. We found that it's not the flu virus that makes you feel miserable, it's your immune system's *response* to the virus that makes you feel miserable.

This breakthrough discovery led to many scientific papers and talks and advanced the cause of medicine. I was honored and pleased to have been a part of it.

But on that Friday morning, I didn't give a damn about any of that. I was exhausted, my entire body ached, I was shaking with chills, and I felt sick to my stomach. I wasn't thinking about science; all I cared about was getting through that last cycle until 2:00 p.m., when I would start to feel better.

Sure enough, by five o'clock that evening I felt completely normal. By six, I felt great. By seven, I was at a party having a wonderful time. Never in my life have I recovered from the flu so quickly, going from trough to peak in just hours. The express-train transformation was spectacular enough that it almost made me want to volunteer for a test trial again.

Almost.

Keeping it Up

MANY YEARS AFTER I CONDUCTED ALL THE RESEARCH with rats, I took a position as a medical officer with the U.S. Food and Drug Administration. I reviewed applications from drug companies who wanted to test or market their experimental drugs in the U.S., and frequently met with their representatives. These meetings were generally dull to those without a science background. We discussed topics like how to document a drug's half-life, or what dose of the drug was to be used in the animal carcinogenicity studies. One meeting, however, was anything but boring.

A company was developing what would have become the first drug in pill form to treat erectile dysfunction. Early clinical trials had produced promising data, and company reps wanted to talk to us about the additional studies and data the FDA required before they could market their drug.

During the meeting, all the company representatives sat on one side of a long conference table, while the FDA officers sat on the other. Everyone maintained a professional attitude during the meeting, even when we discussed the "efficacy endpoint," or results, the drug would have to achieve to show it worked. The efficacy endpoint we eventually agreed upon was "Get it up, keep it up, and get it in." It took some restraint, but no one snickered.

All was going quite well until one member of the FDA group unexpectedly made a demand no one had anticipated. The officer was not from my division, but from the section that reviewed all blood-level data.

"It's standard procedure to obtain blood levels during trials," he said. "If you want the FDA's approval, you need to get blood levels at the efficacy endpoint."

He didn't crack a smile. No one said anything for a few awkward seconds. A few eyebrows went up on the other side of the table.

For any other study, the request would've been routine. Obtaining drug levels during a clinical trial is done all the time; the FDA generally doesn't approve a drug without comparing pre- and post-drug blood levels to gauge a drug's effectiveness. For example, in a trial for narcotics, a doctor would infuse a narcotic into a patient, and then draw blood while the patient's pain is decreasing; a test would show if the drug's effectiveness correlated with the blood levels it achieved. The blood drawing for narcotic trials are no problem, since the patient is usually lying in a hospital bed.

For this study, however, we had all assumed the drug would be tested in the privacy of the patient's bedroom. To draw blood at the "efficacy endpoint" would mean—

I immediately focused my mind on something pleasant. I visualized the time I drove the green on the par-four eighteenth hole at the Eden Course in St. Andrews, Scotland. I pictured the sunsets on St. Croix in the Virgin Islands. I even concentrated on a mental image of a large, frosty glass of beer. I tried to picture anything but a middle-aged couple rolling around in a bed having passionate sex, while a phlebotomist attempted to stick a needle into one of the man's veins and withdraw a blood sample.

I glanced sideways at some of my colleagues, who looked like they too were trying to focus on something else. I looked across the table at the company reps who were processing what the FDA official was saying. Some of the eyebrows were still up. I assumed they were considering the difficulty of finding couples who would agree to participate in such a study.

The meeting eventually ended a little awkwardly, and the company reps didn't commit to any specific plan. We all went off to our offices, some of us in groups, and we only discussed the strange blood-level request once the doors were closed.

"Can you imagine what a subject is going to say to his wife?" one colleague said, laughing.

"Sure," responded another. "'Honey, I've got some good news and some bad news. The good news is they've come up with a cure for my impotence, and they're going to give me the pills! The bad news is we're going to have some company.'"

Fortunately, the FDA eventually agreed to a more reasonable study design, and couples were allowed to celebrate their efficacy endpoint in private. Today, multiple erectile dysfunction drugs are readily available. Whenever I see one of those ubiquitous ads, I can't help but remember the time I drove the green on the par-four eighteenth hole at St. Andrews...

Part V
The Major

1988-1990

I'm in the
Army Now!

A FTER EIGHT AND A HALF YEARS in Cincinnati, it was time for me to leave and take a faculty position somewhere. Most board-certified surgeons with two doctoral degrees teach at a medical school, but I chose a different route. After interviewing at a number of schools, another offer caught my fancy: the world-renowned U.S. Army Institute for Surgical Research wanted me to work for them as a surgeon and chief of surgical studies at their burn center.

Although the pay would be substantially less than a professor's, I took the job for a number of reasons. First, it offered a chance to serve my country. Second, the research opportunities would be excellent—the burn unit provided cutting-edge surgical services. Finally, I had grown tired of frigid temperatures. I was born and raised in the South, so the winters in Ohio seemed interminable. The chance to live in the sun-soaked climate of San Antonio, Texas, was certainly enticing.

I left Cincinnati on December 31, 1987, in the middle of an unrelenting, bone-chilling blizzard. Three days later I arrived in San Antonio, where the temperature was a balmy 72°F. The sun gently thawed me, and I was relaxed and blissful—here it was January 3, and I was eating lunch outside in a short-sleeve shirt! And to top it all off, I marveled, I was now in the Army. I was thoroughly delighted to be in San Antonio.

Before joining the Army, my only familiarity with the military experience came from two sources: my father, who told me stories from his

World War II Army days, and a senior surgery resident at the hospital where I had interned, who had been a Navy corpsman prior to enrolling in medical school. My dad taught me Army tricks, like how to cool a can of beer when it's hot and you have no refrigeration: stick the can in a wet sock. As the water evaporates, it cools the beer.

The senior resident, on the other hand, shared his favorite stories of being a corpsman in Vietnam. He was assigned to a small forward base, where he and a very junior physician made up the entire medical team. The physician had been drafted right after completing his internship, and he did not appreciate having the war interrupt his residency. He also resented the military activities the Army thought he should perform. He was a physician, dammit, not a soldier.

The U.S. Army, of course, thought otherwise. And to add insult to injury, not only did the young doctor have to shoot rifles, march, and salute, he also had to complete paperwork—and the Army had a jaw-dropping boatload of it.

There were forms on how many patients he had treated. There were forms on how many supplies he had used. There were forms on the general sanitation of his unit. There were forms on how many forms he had filled out.

At first, the doctor just ignored the forms. Eventually, a superior officer called and threatened him with severe consequences if he didn't complete them—such as having his one-year tour in Vietnam extended. He begrudgingly started complying, but found a way to get his superior back for requiring a doctor to perform such a menial, mind-numbing task.

He created a form of his own and entitled it "Rodent Control Report." He diagrammed the camp on a piece of graph paper and made a notation of every location in the camp where a rat had been seen during the previous month. He then included this "report" with all the other forms he had to forward to headquarters each month.

Eventually, this doctor was rotated back to the States, and replaced by an Army physician who actually wanted to be an Army physician. The new doctor took great pride in doing everything strictly by the book, especially the meticulous completion of all the required forms.

For the first three months of this new physician's tour, everything went smoothly and his superior officers had no complaints. Then one day he got an irate call from headquarters, demanding to know why he was three months behind in his rodent control reports.

The doctor, horrified that he'd missed a form, scrambled to find it. He soon realized it didn't exist, but he wasn't about to ask headquarters any questions. Instead, he dutifully prepared and submitted his own rodent control reports for the remainder of his tour.

How Not
to Salute

I F YOU WANT TO JOIN THE ARMY, you need to attend a special
training course first. For enlisted personnel, this course is referred to
as "basic training" or "boot camp." Those who wish to become commissioned officers but didn't graduate from West Point or take ROTC in
college must attend the U.S. Army's Officer Candidate School. Unofficially, soldiers refer to OCS as either "charm school" or "salute school,"
since that's where candidates learn essential information like how and
whom to salute. The course was 10 weeks long when I enlisted.

The day I arrived in San Antonio, after enjoying that peaceful lunch in
the sun, I got a call saying the burn unit needed me immediately. A Marine
Corps helicopter had crashed, leaving a dozen Marines seriously burned.
Other recent accidents had occurred involving Army and Air Force personnel, also resulting in a large number of burn victims. Because the Army
burn center is the sole facility caring for combat burn casualties within the
entire U.S. military, all members of the armed forces who are burned are
sent there for care. We also received all the local civilian burn victims from
the San Antonio area, plus residents of Texas who had no insurance. Sometimes, important foreign officials who had severe burns were transferred to
us. The net effect of all this was that on January 3, 1988, the unit was
overflowing with critically burned patients.

The commander of the unit could send me to salute school for the next
two and a half months, or he could send me to the burn unit to help take

care of the patients. Since I was already a fully trained burn surgeon, this wasn't a difficult choice. He had our head sergeant, Sgt. Bobby Marr, officially note that I had completed the OCS course, and on January 11, 1988, I went from Dr. Waymack to Major Waymack. I'm proud to say I'm one of the very few field-grade officers in the history of the U.S. Army who have never been to any form of salute school.

Ironically, I was the least-military officer in the entire U.S. Army. Within the Army, the Medical Corps is considered the least military of all the Corps. Within the Medical Corps, the Research and Development Command is considered the least-military command. Within the Research and Development Command, the Institute for Surgical Research is considered the least military. And within the Institute, I ended up being the least-military officer.

Sergeant Marr figured I was a quick study.

"Everything you need to know about being an officer is in this manual," he said, handing me a thick book. "Read it, and you'll be fine. No one will ever know you didn't go to OCS."

"Yes, sir!" I exclaimed.

He shook his head slowly and reconsidered his last statement.

"No, Major. I'm a master sergeant and you're an officer, so I call *you* 'sir,'" he explained. "You just call me 'Sergeant.' Also, don't ever salute enlisted personnel first."

I knew I had a lot to learn.

The book was the *Army Officer's Guide*, a manual of practical advice and information on Army leadership and command. For the next month, instead of reading the *Annals of Surgery* or the *Journal of Burn Care & Research* when I got home, I would study the officer's manual. There was an awful lot of very specific information on, for example, having the correct military style and dress, how to speak (say "yes, sir" and "no, sir" if you're addressing an officer), and when to salute. I studied hard and felt pretty comfortable with Army jargon, expectations, and even how to identify ranks.

I did have trouble, though, with the endless array of foreign medical officers who visited the burn unit. None of them had the same insignias of rank that the U.S. Armed Forces used. Most of them had stars on their shoulders, which in our military system denotes a general or admiral. It turns out that stars are a dime a dozen in most other armed forces, which I learned after I saluted a two-star, distinguished-looking officer from a country in South America. Hell, I thought he was a damn major general! How was I to know he was only a measly captain? After that embarrassing incident, I adopted a new game plan. Whenever I saw an officer from a foreign country headed my way, I turned and walked in the opposite direction as fast as possible.

One day as I was leaving the hospital, I saw what looked like a U.S. Army officer headed my way. He had on a green uniform that looked exactly like mine did from a distance. Recognizing that he was in the U.S. Army, I paid particular attention to what insignia was on his shoulders. Anything below the rank of major, I would wait for him to salute first. Anything above the rank of major, I would salute first. If he were another major, we'd just smile and say hello—my perpetual hope.

As the officer approached, I noted that the insignia was silver. This narrowed the choices of rank down to first lieutenant, captain, lieutenant colonel, colonel, or general. I calculated that the odds were fifty-fifty that I would initiate the salute, and it's a real faux pas in the military if you're the one who's supposed to salute first and don't—especially if you're a major and should know better.

I squinted and focused on the shape of the insignia, which looked like a diamond. There was no diamond-shaped insignia in the officer's manual. I started to get a little nervous. Finally, I gave up. At a distance of about ten feet, I beat him to a salute by half a second. His face turned a deep red and he looked down as he passed me.

At unit headquarters, I found Sergeant Marr at his desk.

"The strangest thing just happened," I said, recounting the story. "What officer has a diamond insignia?"

He groaned and did a face-plant on his desk.

"Major, you just saluted a ROTC," he replied. (Pronounced "rotsi," the acronym stands for Reserve Officer Training Corps, an organization for college students in the U.S. who are training to be military officers while earning their degrees.)

"But they're not really officers," I replied.

Sergeant Marr looked at me and sighed.

"That's right, sir," he said, with a look on his face that was somewhere between pity and exasperation.

In my defense, a visiting general made a far worse blunder when he stopped by the burn unit one day to visit an injured Marine.

The Marines look after each other, and often seem like the world's largest family. Whenever one of them was admitted to our unit, you could count on an endless stream of visitors, including high-ranking officers. Naturally, the visits did wonders for the patient's morale. After all, if you were a private and a general stopped by to visit you—even though there's no Marine Corps base within hundreds of miles of San Antonio—you'd feel pretty special!

One time, a Marine Corps helicopter crashed in Korea, and ten Marines were critically burned. As soon as we were alerted to their impending arrival, we scrambled to make room in the burn center's already-full intensive care unit. In the few hours between when the U.S. Air Force plane left Korea and when it arrived at our hospital, we moved all the ICU patients but two to the burn ward, freeing up beds for the incoming Marines.

Of the two exceptions, one was an elderly woman who was too sick to move. The other was an illegal alien from Mexico. A couple of days earlier, "Juan" had managed to swim up the Gulf of Mexico, around the border, and into the U.S. Once ashore, and exhausted from his swim along the coast, Juan fell asleep in an abandoned structure. It caught fire during the night, engulfing Juan and burning him badly. Since he had no medical insurance, the first hospital to which he was taken promptly transferred him to us.

Juan's injuries were severe. Half his skin had been burned off, and he had suffered severe smoke inhalation. We immediately placed him on a ventilator to help his damaged lungs breathe. INS soon showed up, and after a brief investigation announced that they would deport Juan following his discharge from the hospital.

Juan spoke no English, but we had many bilingual personnel at the hospital. The bigger problem was that he couldn't speak a word of anything with an endotracheal tube down his throat, connecting him to the ventilator. All he could do was nod or shake his head.

When the Marines arrived, they filled the remaining ten beds in the burn ICU. We began various treatments, including surgical excisions of their burn wounds and ventilator care for those with smoke inhalation injuries.

Two days after the burned Marines arrived, the commandant of the Marine Corps, Gen. Alfred M. Gray Jr., arrived to see his men. A large team of our unit's personnel greeted the four-star general, who arrived in the ICU with an entourage of colonels, captains, and noncommissioned officers (NCOs). After the perfunctory introductions and handshakes, the general was anxious to check on his Marines.

One of our colonels took General Gray to the door outside the first Marine's room. The sign on the door read "Pvt. John Smith, U.S. Marine Corps, 45% burn." The colonel described Private Smith's injuries, explained the operation we'd performed, and told the general we would inspect the skin grafts in two days.

When the colonel was done speaking, General Gray clicked his heels together.

"Colonel, I want to meet this Marine," he said in an authoritative voice.

Nurses quickly put a cap, mask, sterile gloves, and surgical gown on the general, so he wouldn't contaminate the patient or the semi-sterile room. General Gray approached Private Smith, and his brisk efficiency disappeared for a minute.

"How are you doing, Private?" he asked kindly. "The Marine Corps is proud of you, son. Is there anything you need?"

The general pinned a Marine Corps medal to the sheets on Private Smith's bed, and his entourage moved on to the next room. After that visit, the colonel led the group past the third room, Juan's, and stopped at the fourth. He began to describe Private Brown's injuries, when he saw that General Gray had stopped at Juan's door.

"Colonel," the general said, nodding his head in Juan's direction. "I want to meet this Marine."

"Sir, he's not a Marine," the colonel explained.

The general didn't seem to hear that clarification.

"Colonel!" he snapped. "I want to meet this Marine. Now!" He entered Juan's room without waiting for permission.

Approaching the bed, General Gray apparently realized he didn't know this poor fellow's name or rank.

"How are you, Lance Corporal?" he asked Juan, guessing. "Err... you *are* a lance corporal, aren't you, Marine?"

Not understanding a word of English, Juan just smiled weakly and nodded yes.

"Oh, of course," General Gray said, noting the tube. "You can't speak with that damned tube down your throat, can you, son?"

Juan smiled and nodded.

"The Marine Corps is proud of you, Lance Corporal," General Gray said. "Are you in much pain? Oh, I'm sorry to hear that. I know about pain, Marine. I was once wounded, too. Received a Purple Heart in Vietnam. But don't worry, son, it'll ease up."

Juan smiled and nodded.

"I've got a medal for you here—let me pin it to your sheets," the general said. "Now, if there's anything you need, you just let us know, okay? Good."

An hour later, the Marine entourage departed the hospital. A few of us doctor-officers stood at attention and saluted, then relaxed once the cars were out of sight.

"Did you guys see the captain just outside the civilian's room?" asked one of the doctors.

"Yeah, it looked like he was reading the patient information," another said, with a hint of a smile.

"I'd be willing to bet good money that captain will never tell General Gray that he gave a Marine Corps medal to an illegal alien," I said. Captains aren't stupid.

"Well, he probably deserved the medal," the first doctor said, shrugging. "I mean, he certainly acted like a Marine. He hit the beach in a foreign country and was wounded."

The following day, a congressman from the U.S. House Armed Services Committee came by to visit the injured Marines and show them his support. The hosting colonel gave him the same tour he had given the general, except when they passed Juan's room, the colonel gestured at the door and said, "And this is Honorary Lance Corporal Juan Gomez."

The congressman stopped.

"What the hell is an honorary lance corporal?" he asked.

The colonel explained. Luckily, the congressman had a sense of humor.

As for Juan, I always wondered if the INS ever deported him. After all, how could you deport a decorated Marine Corps hero?

The Nimrod Award

WILD BILL WAS A TRAUMA SURGEON with me in the Army Burn Unit. His real name was Col. William McManus, and he'd been a policeman and fireman in his pre-doctor life. After medical school and a surgery residency, he joined the Army and was based in the burn unit. For seventeen years, he was chief of the clinical division at the U.S. Army Institute of Surgical Research.

Wild Bill had several stories about one of our colleagues, a surgeon in the burn unit. One fall, the surgeon wanted to try deer hunting. As he had never been hunting before, he brought along a noncommissioned officer (NCO) who was an expert hunter. Based on the NCO's advice, the surgeon bought a rifle from a local sporting goods store, and the two of them headed out into the hill country of Texas on the first day of deer season.

They hiked through brush for several hours without seeing a single deer. When they came upon a wood fence that bordered private property, the surgeon climbed over, despite the NCO's warnings that it wasn't a good idea.

"Look!" the surgeon suddenly exclaimed. "A deer!"

He raised his rifle and took aim.

"Sir, that's not a deer!" the NCO hollered, from behind the fence.

The surgeon ignored him and fired, and the animal fell to the ground. He raced through pasture to inspect his prize, with the NCO close behind.

When they reached the animal, they found an angry rancher standing over his dead goat.

"What the hell were you thinking, dumb-ass?" the rancher bellowed. "That's one of my prize goats!"

The surgeon looked at the goat with a bewildered look.

"I could've sworn that was a deer," he said. "It had antlers."

The rancher looked at him in disbelief.

"You're paying for my goat, ya stupid idiot," he said, eyes narrowing. "I'm keeping your rifle until you come back here with cash. Now get off my property!"

The surgeon, deflated, turned around and headed back to the fence.

"With your goat!" the rancher roared. "If you're going to shoot my animal, you better damn well dispose of him!"

The NCO told the surgeon he'd take care of it and dragged the dead goat back to his pickup truck. The surgeon drove home with his tail between his legs. Meanwhile, the NCO drove back to the burn center and showed the commander the two-point buck the surgeon had bagged.

A few weeks later at a regularly scheduled awards ceremony, our commanding officer presented some citations and medals to various personnel. At the end of the presentation, the commander asked the surgeon to come up for a special award. Surprised and pleased, he got up and walked to the podium. He was horrified to have the CO recount the story, then hand him what he referred to as the "Nimrod Award": two goat horns mounted on a plaque.

That same surgeon unofficially received another Nimrod Award some years later.

Our commander received an unusual phone call from the Pentagon one day. He was used to getting calls from the Pentagon and U.S. military installations all over the world, and every once in a while he'd get a phone call from the White House, but this one was different.

Pentagon:	Colonel! This is General Smith at the Pentagon.
Colonel:	Yes, sir! How can I help you, sir?
Pentagon:	Order that #$&8@ surgeon of yours to remove his curse immediately! We have a diplomatic crisis with grave international consequences thanks to him!
Colonel:	Excuse me, sir?

Our CO quickly found out that one of his surgeons had done something catastrophically unprofessional. The surgeon was from a Middle Eastern country but had immigrated to the U.S. after finishing his medical training. He joined the Army and was assigned to the burn unit as a surgeon.

From time to time, our allies send their military surgeons to our unit in San Antonio to be trained in burn care. On one occasion, the ally was a Middle Eastern country near our surgeon's country of origin. Since the two men were both from the same part of the world, our commander naturally assigned our surgeon to be the visiting surgeon's host and mentor. Well, as they say, it seemed like a good idea at the time.

One day, the two surgeons got into a heated argument and—despite two college degrees, two medical school degrees, and two surgery residencies between them—it devolved to a thoroughly irrational, petty squabble over something insignificant. In the heat of passion, our surgeon told the visiting surgeon that he was placing a curse on him and the next seven generations of his family.

Despite all his scientific education, the visiting surgeon was horrified. He called his embassy in Washington, D.C., told them of the awful curse placed on him and his future descendants, and asked the embassy personnel to help. Outraged by the insult, the ambassador himself called the U.S. State Department and demanded that the U.S. Army surgeon take back his curse.

The State Department then called the Pentagon. (I am not making this up.) Next, the Pentagon called our CO, who called the offending surgeon into his office.

As the conversation between the two was behind closed doors, those of us outside his office are only certain of two things: one, the conversation was clearly one-sided, and two, the CO wasn't whispering. Immediately after this private meeting, the commander gathered the burn unit personnel—including the visiting surgeons—and the offending surgeon publicly and apologetically removed the curse. No one was more relieved than the visiting surgeon, except possibly our commander.

The PT Test

THOSE WHO SERVE IN THE ARMED FORCES are not only supposed to dress and act in a very specific way, but they are also supposed to be in excellent physical shape. That requirement is not waived for personnel in non-combat units such as the Medical Corps.

In March, after I'd been in the Army a couple of months, I learned that I needed to pass the semi-annual PT (physical training) test in May. All active-duty personnel my age must be able to do fifty pushups, followed by fifty sit-ups, followed by a two-mile run within sixteen minutes. I thought those requirements were ridiculous, and said so.

"What happens if I fail the test?" I asked Sergeant Marr.

He raised an eyebrow and shook his head.

"Doc, you don't want to fail the test," he responded. "If you do, you have to show up every morning at 0600 to do PT drills."

Thus motivated, I began to prepare for the test. Every evening when I got back from the hospital, I did fifty pushups and fifty sit-ups. Then I'd have a cold beer and curse the training. I'd crush the can with my now-muscular hands, then run two miles in less than sixteen minutes. By the end of April, I was easily completing the required activities on a daily basis.

PT testing began the first Monday in May, at 0600 sharp. You could take it every morning if you wanted, but you only had to pass it once to be cleared for another six months. I showed up with about a hundred other soldiers, but since I was the highest-ranking officer there, I let everyone else go first. Most passed the pushup and sit-up part, but a few didn't and promptly left. Finally my turn came. I did the required fifty pushups, then rolled over and did the required fifty sit ups.

"Congratulations, sir!" said the sergeant running the PT testing. "You passed the first part."

I relaxed and lay back on the grass, breathing heavily.

"Okay everyone, four laps around the half-mile course starting NOW!" the sergeant hollered.

Huh? Where was my beer break?! No wonder everyone wanted to go before me. They had now had a rest period and I hadn't, and I was the oldest one in the entire group. Still struggling for breath, I started out on the course in a slow jog.

Each time I finished a lap, the sergeant barked out the time. When I finished the first mile, I was chagrined to hear it had taken eight minutes; I'd been running a seven-and-a-quarter-minute mile while training. I pushed myself as hard as I could, and my legs felt like Jell-O as I finished the second mile in a sprint.

"Seven minutes fifteen seconds!" the sergeant called, looking at his stopwatch. "Total time: fifteen point two five. Congratulations, sir! You passed."

I collapsed to the ground and squeezed my eyes shut, panting.

"Great," I said, trying to slow my breathing down.

I finally got up after a minute, and started to head back to my apartment for a shower.

"Sir, I can do your weigh-in whenever you want," the sergeant said.

"What weigh-in?" I asked, stopping.

"Oh, I thought you knew. We have to weigh you and measure your height," he explained. "If you're too heavy for your height, you fail and you still have to do the 0600 hours training every morning."

He took a second to look me up and down, as though he were appraising a pig at a state fair.

"Nah, you won't fail," he said confidently.

By that afternoon, I had finished an operation on a burned soldier and was back in the lab conducting some animal research with Sergeant Guzman assisting.

"How'd you do on the test, Sarge?" I asked him.

"Maximum score!" he said proudly.

We worked side by side, mostly silently, while we conducted our tests. I sensed something was wrong.

"You okay?" I asked. "Just tired from the run?"

"Aw, I'm fine," he responded. "I'm just worried about my buddy, Sergeant Horatio." He cocked his head in the direction of the next lab over.

"He got a perfect score too, but he failed because he's ten pounds too heavy and his neck is half an inch too small."

Huh?

"What the hell does neck size have to do with physical fitness?" I asked.

"Well, if you're too heavy for your height, they measure your neck and waist, to see if you're heavy because you're muscular," Sergeant Guzman explained. "According to the Army's chart, for his body weight Horatio's neck has to be sixteen inches around to be classified as 'muscular,' and his is only fifteen and a half."

That seemed ridiculous to me.

I liked Sergeant Horatio and thought he was an excellent soldier and lab assistant. I immediately came up with a plan, and had Horatio come over to our lab.

"Sergeant," I said, putting my hand on his shoulder, "you're going to retake the PT test tomorrow morning, and you're going to pass it. Meet me here at 0530."

"Yes, sir," he responded, looking a little confused.

The next morning I met Horatio in the lab. I had a one-liter bag of salt solution, a large syringe, a long needle, and some alcohol swabs. He looked quite concerned when I explained I was going to inject the salt solution into his neck.

"Do you trust me, soldier?" I asked, looking him in the eye.

He hesitated for a second.

"Yes, sir?" he answered. It sounded more like a question, but he didn't flinch when I injected him with the long needle.

At 0600 hours, Sergeant Horatio took the PT test and once more did extremely well on the pushups, sit-ups, and two-mile run. He then returned with everyone else to the main office for the weigh-in. Sergeant Marr shook his head when he saw Horatio.

"Sergeant, unless you've lost ten pounds since yesterday, you're not going to pass," he said, a little impatiently.

Horatio stripped down for height and weight measurements.

Sergeant Marr read the numbers.

"I told you," he said. "You're still overweight."

"Could you please measure my waist and neck?" Horatio asked.

Sergeant Marr shrugged and got out his tape measure, then wrapped it around Horatio's thick midsection.

"No change." He measured his neck, looked at the number, then measured it again.

"What the hell?" he said, looking at the tape measure. "Sixteen and a half inches? Well, I guess you pass, Horatio."

Sergeant Horatio glanced at me and looked as pleased as could be.

I didn't feel too bad about helping a good soldier get around an unreasonably fastidious requirement. After all, I was the least-military officer in the Army, so how was I to know?

Cannon Cockers

MEMBERS OF THE ARMED FORCES are not only expected to be in excellent physical shape, they're also obligated to be experts in the use of rifles, pistols, and other types of firearms. Happily, weapons training was optional for certain non-combat units, and Medical Corps personnel were some of the lucky ones exempt from this requirement. Those of us in the burn unit referred to the regular U.S. Army units, somewhat condescendingly, as "cannon cockers."

There was a time, though, when even doctors had to pass the marksmanship course.

This was a couple of decades before my service in the burn unit. Back in the 1960s, all medical personnel had to participate in a day of target-practice shooting at Camp Bullis, some twenty miles away from our base at Fort Sam Houston in San Antonio. During those sessions, the unit maintained a perfect record: they never once accidentally shot each other.

One year, the exercise took place in the middle of the summer, when the temperature was over 100°F. After an afternoon of shooting cacti, sand, rocks, small rodents, and, occasionally, the official army targets, the medical personnel in the burn unit were hot, tired, and thirsty. As they loaded the bus for the trip back to Fort Sam Houston, someone suggested they stop along the way for a cold beer. Most unit commanders in the U.S. Army would have frowned upon such a suggestion, but the burn unit commander thought it was an excellent idea. He had the bus driver pull into the parking lot of the first bar they passed, and everyone settled down to a cold one.

Unfortunately, this wasn't just any bar. The Army has a list of institutions its personnel are prohibited from frequenting, such as bars that have taken financial advantage of the servicemen or have inappropriate entertainment, like nude female dancers. This was one such bar.

Meanwhile, on the highway outside, a military car carrying two Army Military Police (MPs) passed by. Upon seeing the U.S. Army bus in the parking lot of an off-limits bar, during normal working hours, the MPs made an abrupt U-turn. Inside, the MPs saw a couple dozen men and women in battlefield dress uniforms seated at a very long table with many pitchers of beer being happily consumed.

One of the MPs walked up to one of the soldiers seated at the table. He took out a pad of paper and cleared his throat loudly. The table quieted down immediately.

"All right soldier, who's your commander?" the MP barked.

The soldier—a surgeon at the burn unit—didn't answer, but turned his head toward the commander at the end of the table. Everyone else turned their heads at the same time. The commander slowly rose from the table.

"I am," he said. "What's the problem?"

The MPs immediately noted the colonel's eagles. Their faces blanched and they stood at attention.

"Nothing, sir. Sorry, sir. All good!"

The MPs rapidly backed out of the bar, and the colonel ordered another round of beer for everyone.

It's not surprising that after incidents such as this, routine marksmanship training was eliminated as one of the requirements for members of the Army's burn unit.

The U.S. Air Force, however, kept the weapons training requirement for medical personnel. While I was stationed at the Army's burn unit, I spent part of my time helping the Air Force liver and kidney transplant team located across town at the Wilford Hall Hospital on Lackland Air Force Base. Because they only had two surgeons, they occasionally needed a third to have a smooth-running liver transplant. Since I was trained to do liver transplants, I volunteered to help them.

They were excellent surgeons, but because they were also airmen, the Air Force wanted them to act like regular military personnel occasionally. In other words, shoot a gun every now and then. The target practice was simple and quick—the surgeons were given a pistol and twelve bullets each, and instructed to simply "fire away" at the target. If they happened to make fourteen points (one point for hitting the target, two points for hitting the bullseye), they would receive marksmanship medals. One of these world-class liver transplant surgeons was a reasonable shot, and usually would get at least eleven of his twelve bullets to hit the target. Unfortunately, he was never able to get enough hits to the inner target to win the award—until one day, when he stood at the firing range and began to fire at the target. The sequence went something like this:

Pulls the trigger	→	Target jumps
Pulls the trigger	→	Target jumps
Pulls the trigger	→	Target jumps
		Target jumps
Pulls the trigger	→	Target jumps
Pulls the trigger	→	Target jumps
		Target jumps

After five shots, my friend put down his pistol and tried to figure out what was happening. How was the target jumping when he wasn't shooting?

He turned to his right just in time to see an Air Force nurse, standing about ten feet away, aim her pistol at her target, which was only a few feet to the right of his target. She closed her eyes, turned her head, flinched, and pulled the trigger. Apparently, she did that every time, so her gun ended up veering off to the left. And about every third time she fired her gun, with her eyes closed and flinching, the bullet went so far to the left that it hit my friend's target.

If he had really been concerned with getting a marksmanship medal, my friend would have asked the NCO in charge of target practice for a new target and twelve new bullets. Because he was more interested in getting back to his sick patients, he didn't bother. He just kept firing bullets at his target.

A few minutes later, everyone on the firing line had emptied their pistols. The NCO in charge collected the targets and counted out loud the points my friend had made during the day's target practice.

"Congratulations, sir! You've finally won your medal!"

My friend wasn't about to remind the NCO that each shooter was only given twelve bullets but his target had fourteen holes, and he accepted his marksmanship medal with a clear conscience.

"I didn't cheat to get it," he explained. "That nurse just helped me out a bit. Besides, the important thing is that we were both able to get back to doing the real thing we've been trained to do: saving lives."

Next Stop, San Antonio

THE LIVER TRANSPORT TEAM was not my only opportunity to interact with the U.S. Air Force during my tour of duty. Because the Army did not fly airplanes, and because ours was the only burn unit for the entire U.S. Armed Forces, the Air Force would fly us to pick up an injured service member from somewhere in the world, then back to our base in San Antonio.

During my years at the University of Cincinnati as a research fellow, I had taken many flights on various airlines to locations all around the world for scientific talks. Those flights had been comfortable, and except for three occasions when passengers had become ill, they had been unremarkable.

Flights on military aircraft, as you might expect, were memorable. Usually I had a critical patient I was trying to save, but it's a little tricky to practice medicine on board a U.S. Air Force transport plane. The engines are so deafening that listening through a stethoscope is pointless, and it's a lot darker inside a jet than inside an operating room or ICU.

Nevertheless, I had a great advantage: there's no fixed flight schedule for an Army major flying on an Air Force plane. If you're the surgeon, the plane doesn't leave until you're on it. In that regard, it's as if you're the President of the United States: you arrive at the airbase to find the plane waiting for you, and the pilot won't take off until you give him the go-ahead. Those who arrive before you are early; those who arrive after you are out of luck. As the surgeon on these mercy flights, standard operating procedure was that I was the last person onto the plane before the ground crew closed the door behind me.

When I came on board, I would find the captain of the plane—usually a captain in the Air Force—waiting by the doorway for me. I would smile and say something in a friendly tone, trying to indicate that I considered him or her to be an equal partner in this medical flight. For example, I would say something informal like, "Thanks for flying us, Captain. Well, next stop Edwards Air Force Base," or "Take us home to San Antonio, please."

Unbeknownst to me, however, on most of these flights I was the de facto commander of the plane. An Army major outranks an Air Force captain, so everyone (but me) considered me to be in charge of the plane, not the captain who was actually flying it. However, because I was 1) not a pilot, and 2) focused on patient care, I would never have presumed to tell the guy flying the plane how or where to fly it.

The particular flight that taught me about the chain of command—yes, I should have learned this in the *Army Officer's Guide*—started out rather routinely. There had been an accident at an Air Force base in California, and an airman had suffered severe burns over about a third of his body. A corpsman and nurse from our unit flew with me to the Air Force base, and an ambulance took us to the base's infirmary. We loaded the airman onto the ambulance and headed back to the plane, where we secured him to a bed inside the Air Force C-9 transport plane. The ground crew then closed the plane's door behind me. I turned to the pilot.

"Next stop San Antonio," I said.

Moments later we were airborne and headed back to San Antonio on what was supposed to be a three-hour flight. It was 2300 San Antonio time when we left California.

About twenty minutes later we were cruising at 33,000 feet. I checked the patient to make sure he was doing okay at the now slightly lower oxygen content. He was alert and his unburned skin was pink, indicating that he had plenty of oxygen in his system despite the lower air pressure.

The nurse and corpsman then gave me a look that I knew meant "Doc, we can handle this—go relax." I stretched out in a nearby seat, and within minutes was sound asleep.

The next thing I remember was the Air Force captain waking me up. He looked very anxious.

"Umm, Major, I know you said to land next in San Antonio, and I've been trying for the past two hours, but the thunderstorms down there are preventing me from safely landing. sir, we're going to run out of fuel soon. Could I please have your permission to divert this plane to Houston to land and refuel?"

I bolted up from my seat.

"Of course!" I exclaimed. "You can land this plane anywhere you damn well feel like. Just get it down!"

The pilot quickly headed back to the cockpit. I followed, thoroughly dumbfounded that we had such an idiot for a pilot.

What the hell was he thinking? I thought, irritated. *What am I, the damn pilot?*

As we headed east towards Houston, I pointed out Interstate Highway 10, which was now visible directly below us.

"Captain, you can land down there," I said, thinking I better stay in the cockpit to give him some direction. It was 0400 so there wasn't much traffic on the highway, and it was straight and flat.

"We're good, sir," the pilot said. "We have just enough fuel to make it to the airport."

We landed safely, refueled, and when the weather cleared in San Antonio, we took off and landed there less than an hour later. As soon as I had made sure the patient was in stable condition at the burn unit, I headed over to headquarters to see Sergeant Marr.

"Sarge, something was wrong with our Air Force pilot," I told him, truly concerned. "He couldn't make any decisions without me! I don't know if he had a brain lapse or lost his confidence, but he just didn't know what to do. It's a good thing I was there!"

Sergeant Marr sighed.

"Major Waymack, didn't you read the manual I gave you?" he asked.

"Well, yeah," I responded. "Sure I did."

"So what happens when a higher-ranking officer gives an order to a lower-ranking officer?" he quizzed.

"They have to follow it!" I answered impatiently, not understanding where he was going with this.

"Major, you were the commander of the flight," Sergeant Marr explained. "Did you tell him to go to San Antonio?"

"Well, sure," I said. "But it's not like I was giving him an order!"

"That's exactly what it was," the sergeant responded. "If you said, 'Next stop San Antonio,' that's a direct order from the commander of the flight."

He sighed and shook his head.

"You almost crashed an Air Force jet, sir."

I thought about that for a moment, puzzled.

"So if I had said, 'Could you please fly us to San Antonio, Captain?' that wouldn't have been an order, and he could have diverted to Houston without my permission?"

"Yes, sir. That's correct. You have to be very precise with your words in the military."

It was a mistake I never repeated. From that day on, I always checked the rank of the pilot when I boarded an Air Force jet. If it turned out that I outranked him or her, I would give them clearance to land the plane anytime and anywhere, without first seeking my permission.

"And that's an order," I would say. Just in case.

The Absent-Minded Colonel

I WAS NOT THE ONLY OFFICER at the Army burn unit who had problems with airplanes. There was one colonel who resembled more an absent-minded professor than an Army officer. He was brilliant in the area of medicine he practiced and had dozens of publications in his field, but he could get lost on a one-way street.

To recognize a lifetime of excellent work, the colonel was invited to give the keynote address at a medical convention in Washington, D.C. The address was to be a review of all the work he had done in his field, and the colonel had spent many days preparing his talk and compiling slides for a presentation.

The keynote address was scheduled at 4:00 p.m. on the next-to-last day of the convention, and over a thousand people were expected to attend. Prior commitments precluded the colonel from attending the first days of the convention, but his secretary found a direct flight from San Antonio that would arrive at Washington National Airport before noon the day of the keynote address. The flight made one quick stop in Nashville, Tennessee.

That morning, the colonel made it onto the correct plane with his slides and some reading material. When the plane landed in Nashville, the pilot gave the standard touchdown announcement: "Ladies and gentlemen, welcome to Nashville International Airport, where the local time is…"

The colonel, who had been preoccupied with his reading, heard the announcement "Welcome to National Airport" and quickly put away his book. Once the plane came to a stop at the airport gate, he got up, grabbed his carry-on bag and slide carousel, and walked off the plane. Inside the terminal, he asked a friendly American Airlines agent where the taxis were, and she pointed him in the right direction.

Eventually he found the taxi line, and jumped in the next cab.

"Morning," the driver said. "Where to?"

"The Washington Hilton," the colonel responded.

The cab driver turned around.

"Sorry, sir, I don't know any hotel by that name around here," he said. "Do you know where it's located?"

"Well, it's downtown," he told the driver patiently. "You know, the big one on Connecticut Avenue."

The driver shook his head slowly.

"Uh, no... I don't know of any street by that name here."

The colonel was perplexed.

"Do you know the city well?" he asked politely. "Maybe you just haven't seen it."

"I've been driving for twenty years, Mister, and I ain't never seen any Connecticut Avenue or Washington Hilton."

The colonel thought for a minute.

Hmmm... perhaps I should get another cab? This fellow doesn't seem to know D.C. very well.

"Sir, are you sure that hotel is in Nashville?" the driver asked. "Maybe it's in another city."

The colonel looked very confused.

"Nashville?" he asked. "Isn't this Washington, D.C.?"

"No, sir," the driver responded. "But I could get you there in about eleven hours. It'll cost about $400, though."

The colonel finally realized what he'd done and hopped out of the cab. He ran back through the airport as fast as he could, pulling his carry-on behind him while holding on to his slide carousel. By the time he got back to the gate, the plane had departed and was on its way to Washington, D.C.

"Don't worry, sir," the gate agent said to the visibly distressed colonel. "There's another flight in four hours, and it will get in at 6:30 p.m."

Sadly, the colonel arrived in D.C. two and a half hours after his keynote address was to have started. This was many years before cell phones were common, and I'm sure he wouldn't have known who to call even if he'd had a phone book and change for a pay phone. I didn't know anyone who had been in the audience at the convention, but I can imagine it must have been a little awkward for the one introducing the absent colonel.

The moral of the story is that if you aren't smart enough to get from point A to point B, you ought to bring along an NCO. They're the ones who have the lion's share of common sense in the military.

The Marvels of Modern Technology

O F COURSE, THERE ARE WORSE THINGS than not showing up for a keynote address. I once witnessed one of those things—or rather, heard it—at a huge convention with academic physicians, drug company researchers, and governmental regulatory agency administrators.

With so many hundreds of people in the audience, the convention hall crew had set up several microphones. One was attached to the speaker's podium, and a few were on stands throughout the hall for questions. But when the first speaker kept walking away from the podium as he talked, the crew realized they needed a portable microphone for those presenters who like to move around.

A member of the electronics team quickly arrived to fix the problem. He clipped a tiny microphone to the speaker's necktie, attached a transmitter the size of a pack of cigarettes to the speaker's belt, and connected a wire between the two. It was bulky and clumsy compared to the sleek, miniature clip-on gadgets that are commonplace today, but in 1988, these portable mics were a marvel of modern technology.

Members of the audience who had never seen a portable microphone before were in awe. No matter where the speaker roamed—and he did seem to traverse the entire auditorium during his talk—we still heard his voice crystal clear.

When the speaker finished, the moderator went to the microphone at the podium and introduced the second lecturer. As the moderator enumerated the lecturer's wonderful accomplishments, those of us in the audience heard another voice.

"Where's the bathroom?" the voice said.

"… is the attending physician in nephrology at Mercy Medical Center in Rockville, New York," the moderator continued.

Then we abruptly heard another voice.

"It's down the hall and to your left, sir," a woman said.

"… and in 1985, he was a diplomat on the American Board of Internal Medicine," the moderator intoned.

The same member of the electronics team who had brought the clip-on microphone quickly left the convention hall and tried chasing down the speaker before he got to the men's room. He eventually succeeded in removing the mic, but not before almost 500 men and women heard the speaker relieving himself in crystal-clear amplified surround sound.

Technology certainly has its pros and cons, doesn't it?

The Mysterious
Briefcase

IN THE DARK AGES BEFORE LAPTOPS and PowerPoint presentations, most medical and scientific talks used simple slides in a revolving carousel. For those who've never seen these ancient relics, slides were color transparencies in a plastic frame. They were essential for conveying scientific information: text slides showed results of experiments and consisted of words, graphs, and numbers; picture slides included microscopic photos of tissues and organs or complex new surgical procedures.

One week, I went to Israel for a conference with other burn surgeons. The meetings were excellent, and surgeon friends who lived in Israel gave me memorable tours of Jerusalem. My friends also recommended some very good restaurants, and I passed these tips on to other surgeons at the conference.

One day between meetings, three plastic surgeons decided to visit one of the recommended restaurants for lunch. One of them would be lecturing that afternoon, so he had a slide carousel filled with fifty slides stored in the briefcase he was carrying. The three surgeons walked from the hotel to the restaurant, had a delicious lunch, then started walking back to the hotel for the afternoon meetings.

They were almost to the hotel when the lecturing surgeon realized he had left his briefcase at lunch. He told his friends to go on without him, and hurried back to the restaurant just twenty minutes after they'd left.

When he arrived, he explained what had happened to the first waiter he saw. The waiter quickly got the manager.

"Ah," said the manager in English. "That was your briefcase?"

"I can't believe I left it!" my friend exclaimed. "Good thing I remembered before my lecture!"

The manager looked solemn.

"I am very sorry to inform you, sir, but your briefcase is, how do you say? Exploded."

It turned out that, this being Jerusalem, an unattended briefcase was always a cause for great alarm. Instead of storing it for a forgetful customer, the restaurant had immediately called the bomb squad. They were at the restaurant within minutes, took the briefcase to a nearby bomb-disposal location, attached an explosive device of their own, and blew it up.

My friend was stunned to find out that the briefcase he had left behind twenty-five minutes earlier was now in a million pieces. He had flown halfway around the world to give a lecture on rebuilding burned hands in children, and now had no slides which would have shown the wonderful surgical techniques he used.

He went ahead with the lecture, and made a valiant effort to explain the techniques without the use of slides or a whiteboard. I'm sure it was the most frustrating lecture he ever gave. After that, he never again left a briefcase or other personal article behind. I think it's safe to say that all of us who were there that day never let our slides out of our sight when we went somewhere to deliver a lecture—even if it was in a relatively safe location like Boise, Idaho.

An Irish
No-Fly Zone

ONE OF THE MANY TRIPS I TOOK while I served in the Army's burn unit was to Belfast, Northern Ireland. Initially, I was supposed to spend two days there as a visiting professor at the Royal Victoria Hospital, part of the Queen's University of Belfast, but the itinerary turned out to include more activities.

I had been a visiting professor before, so I was looking forward to the trip. The assignment is quite stress-free: you give a couple of lectures, make rounds with the residents, and offer advice on their cases. You have some meals with the residents and some with the attending surgeons. Sometimes you're even entertained: this trip, a round of golf at Royal County Down was on the itinerary.

Because I was a U.S. Army officer, and because it was 1989, I needed permission from the British military to visit Northern Ireland. It was supposed to be just a technicality. The commander of the burn unit had Sergeant Marr contact the Pentagon, then the Pentagon informed NATO, NATO informed the British, the British informed the military commander for Northern Ireland, and the commander for Northern Ireland sent the request to his highest-ranking British Army physician for approval, who was supposed to just say "fine." He approved it, but under one condition: that I spend time with British forces in Belfast.

At the time, the ever-present political troubles in Northern Ireland were quite nasty. The Irish Republican Army (IRA) had fought for Irish independence for a couple of centuries, but in 1986 things got much worse. The Irish People's Liberation Organization (IPLO) formed as a Catholic paramilitary group by disaffected and expelled members of the Irish National Liberation Army (INLA). Other disaffected followers of Sinn Fein, another group that advocated violence to achieve their objectives, set up a rival party and military wing.

Yes, it was all very confusing. All I knew was that Catholics and Protestants were killing each other, and the British Army was right in the middle—trying to stop the killing, and getting killed in the process. Several of the paramilitary organizations were not only shooting British soldiers, but were rumored to have obtained surface-to-air missiles to shoot down British helicopters.

I got a phone call from Fort Jericho, the nearby British Army fort, soon after I arrived at my hotel in Belfast.

"Good day, Major!" the caller said cheerfully. "This is Captain Nottingham at Fort Jericho. Welcome to Belfast!"

"Why, thank you, Captain!" I responded. "I'm very happy to be here."

"Well, I hope that remains the case tomorrow, sir," he said brightly. "In light of the current, er, difficulties in Belfast, you can arrive at the fort tomorrow in one of two ways."

He explained that he could send an armored personnel carrier (APC) to pick me up in the morning. This vehicle was sufficiently armored so as to withstand gunshots, Molotov cocktails, and other weaponry currently aimed at British forces. However, he warned me that they had reason to believe that the IRA now possessed some weapons that could pierce the armor.

The second option for coming to the fort in the morning was to take a cab to within a block of the fort's entrance. Then I would walk past the fort on the far side of the street, and stand for exactly one minute at 0900 hours, during which time the British soldiers would confirm my identity. I explained to the caller that I would almost certainly be the only 6'5" male wearing a navy blue suit, white shirt, and red tie, but he insisted they would need the full minute. Then, after receiving the go-ahead signal from the fort, I was to dash inside.

I weighed the options and chose #2, which seemed less likely to get me killed.

The next morning all went according to plan, and I was safely within the fort at 0900. It looked like an old castle, with fifteen-foot walls of concrete and stone, covered on the inside with curious little divots. The highest-ranking British Army surgeon, Lieutenant Colonel McGonagle, welcomed me into his office and introduced me to Army Sergeant Major Fitzroy, a very high-ranking NCO, who gave me a two-hour tour of the historic fort.

Recognizing that the British Army is probably second in strength only to the U.S. Army and maybe the Australian Army, I was determined to act in as military a manner as possible in front of this important sergeant. I walked as though I were marching: chin up, back as straight as a rod, knees smartly up, arms slightly swaying in time, and in as straight a line as possible. Nonetheless, I got the distinct impression I was irritating him. When we got outside the buildings and were in the open part of the fort, he kept his eyes up and serpentined quickly toward the covered part. I followed behind him, walking rigidly upright and in a perfectly straight line.

He saw what I was doing and grabbed my arm, pulling me toward the buildings.

"Bloody hell, man!" he exclaimed, exasperated. "Pardon my language, sir, but don't you know there are snipers up there?"

Actually, no, I didn't. He softened somewhat, realizing I was just an ignorant American.

"You can't walk in a straight line outside the buildings, sir," he explained. "Serpentine! IRA snipers are hiding in the hills directly overlooking this fort, and they'll shoot if they see an easy target."

Ah, that explains the divots, I thought. *They're where the snipers missed their targets.*

For the remainder of my time at the fort, whenever I was outside of the individual buildings, I slouched over and walked like a drunken sailor, darting side to side so as to make it difficult for the snipers to hit me. All the while I kept asking myself, *Who in the hell thought this was a good idea?*

Just before lunch, the commanding officer greeted me.

"Jolly good news!" the lieutenant colonel said enthusiastically.

After dodging potential gunshots for the past couple of hours, I was ready for some good news.

"Major Waymack, I know how pleased you will be," he said, delighted. "At 1500 hours we are going to take you on a helicopter ride over the area."

In light of my extensive experience treating burn victims from helicopter crashes, rotary-wing aircraft are not my preferred method of travel.

"Oh, how lovely!" I responded.

The British officer rubbed his hands together in excitement.

"Of course, I should warn you of one thing," he cautioned, his smile fading. "Generally, the IRA merely fires rifles at us as we fly by. Usually, they miss. However, we have reason to believe the IRA now possesses surface-to-air missiles, compliments of Colonel Qaddafi, and it is possible, although unlikely, they may try to shoot down one of our helicopters with the missiles. In such an event, it would undoubtedly yield a most unfavorable outcome for you."

I must've looked a bit startled.

"So of course, if you would rather not go, we would of course understand," he said. He looked at me expectantly.

You're representing the U.S. Army, I said to myself. *What would General MacArthur do?*

"No problem," I said cheerfully. "It sounds like fun."

"Brilliant!" the officer exclaimed.

We had lunch and toured the base's hospital. At 1445 hours, Lieutenant Colonel McGonagle took a phone call in his office and returned with a look of grave disappointment.

"Major Waymack, I have some very bad news," he said, crestfallen. "The commanding general for Northern Ireland adamantly refused permission to fly you over the area. He said he was not going to be put in a position of having to explain to the Pentagon how we got you killed. So the trip is off. I am so sorry."

He couldn't have looked any more deflated.

"Oh, what a shame!" I said. "You can't believe how much I was looking forward to that flight."

"Well," he said, looking terribly embarrassed, "we have arranged for some tea. I hope that will somewhat compensate you."

"Certainly," I responded graciously. "I very much enjoy British tea."

Later that afternoon, I turned down the commander's offer of an armored personnel carrier and instead just snuck out of the fort, glancing furtively in both directions. After nervously serpentining for a couple of blocks, I hailed a cab back to my hotel. I headed straight for the bar and downed a couple of shots of Irish whiskey. Finally, after half an hour, I relaxed. Upon reflection, I concluded that I was never meant to be a hero, and probably not an Army officer, either.

Stealing Time

DURING MY TIME AT THE BURN UNIT, Sergeant Marr and I became very good friends. We spent many hours discussing the needs of our soldiers, played golf every once in a while, and he even told me I would make a good commander for our unit. But I also looked to him for problem solving, as he was always ready to help whenever I needed something.

One day a new piece of equipment arrived for the animal operating room. It was the size of a pencil, and one tip was a cautery tool that would stop minor bleeding in rats. It was essential for the experimental operations I was performing on them.

The rats were all ready for their operations, so I eagerly opened the box as soon as it arrived. Unfortunately, the tool required a double-A battery, and I couldn't find any in the animal operating room or in the lab. I was about to drive over to the PX and buy one, but stopped by Sergeant Marr's desk on the way to see if he had any.

"What do you need, Doc?" he asked.

"You got any double-A batteries?" I responded. "I need one for a cautery instrument in the animal OR."

"Nah, I just looked for some yesterday," he said. "But I can order them for you. How many do you need?"

"Only one. How long until they arrive?"

Sergeant Marr frowned.

"Well Doc, with all the paperwork it takes to get supplies, it'll be about six weeks."

"Hell, I'm not going to wait that long!" I exclaimed. "That's ridiculous.

The rats are ready, and a double-A battery's less than a buck. I'll just go to the PX and buy one now."

"Hold on, Doc," he said. "I don't want you spending your own money, and you've got better things to do with your time."

He looked pensive for a few seconds, then got up.

"Double A, correct?"

"Yup, that's correct." I followed him as he got up and started walking.

He peaked into the adjutant's office and found it empty. The adjutant, a lieutenant colonel, was the highest-ranking member of the unit who wasn't a physician. He was an administrator, and he and Sergeant Marr strongly disliked each other.

Sergeant Marr walked in to the office and took down the clock that was hanging on the wall. He brought it back to his desk, took out a screwdriver, and removed the back of the clock. Inside were four double-A batteries.

"How many did you say you needed?" he asked.

"Just one."

"Oh what the hell," he said. "Take all four."

He took out all the batteries and handed them to me. He replaced the back of the clock and put it back on the wall in the adjutant's office.

I looked at him with my eyebrows raised.

"Doc, don't worry about it," he said, patting me on the arm. "It won't be a problem."

I put one of the batteries into the cautery instrument and conducted the animal operations that afternoon. A few hours later, I headed over to the coffee maker next to Sergeant Marr's desk.

"How'd the operations go, Doc?" he asked.

"Oh, just great!" I said, pouring myself a cup. "Thanks for your help."

"Sergeant Marr, get in here!" The adjutant sounded very displeased.

Uh-oh, I thought. *It seemed like a good idea at the time...*

Sergeant Marr gave me an exasperated look, got up from his desk, and walked into the adjutant's office.

"What's the problem, sir?"

"I think my clock is broken," the lieutenant colonel said, frowning.

"Hmmm," Sergeant Marr said, taking the clock down. "Sir, I think it's your batteries. You need new batteries."

"Well, are you sure?"

The sergeant fiddled with the clock and nodded.

"Yup. I'm pretty sure that's the problem."

"Well, how long will it take to get new batteries?"

"Oh, with all the paperwork, about six weeks."

"Damn!" The adjutant was very peeved.

Sergeant Marr brought the clock out to his desk and hung it on a hook above his file drawer, where for six weeks it gave him great satisfaction. He didn't really need a reminder that NCOs have a lot more common sense than most officers, but still, it made him smile every time he saw it.

As Seen on TV

YOU CAN'T BE A SURGEON WHO SPECIALIZES IN BURNS and trauma without dealing with the press. It's impossible. Whenever there's a fire and someone gets burned, the media want to know what's happening. If it's someone important who was injured, or if it was a small child, they want you to hold a press conference. Frequently, the family wants that information released to the public, so I've appeared on TV many times. Usually I just respond to questions about how a patient is doing, but one experience was quite different.

It all began one day with a phone call from Alaska in September 1991, when I was the assistant chief of staff at the Shriners Burn Institute, and on the faculty at University of Texas Medical Branch.

Me:	Paul Waymack here.
Caller:	Hello Dr. Waymack, this is Dr. Ted Mala, calling from the Institute for Circumpolar Health Studies in Anchorage.
Me:	(thinking) *There's an office for polar medicine? Seriously?* Yes, hello. How can we help you?
Dr. Mala:	We've got a Russian boy who has suffered serious burns from a fire. Could you folks provide free care for him? He lives in Magadan, a seaport in Siberia.
Me:	Um, well, the hospital would probably be willing to provide free care, but we don't have a jet to pick him up. That would be a pretty expensive private flight.

Dr. Mala: What if I found someone willing to pay for the boy's
                   transport? Would you provide free care then?
Me: Sure. Absolutely.

I couldn't imagine he was going to find the $20K or so needed for that kind of transportation. If he had severe burns, you couldn't just buy the boy a ticket on a commercial airliner.

A couple of hours later, my phone began to ring. First, Senator Ted Stevens of Alaska, calling from Washington, D.C., wanted to thank us for agreeing to provide free care. Then the Soviet Embassy in Washington, D.C., called to thank us. Then Dr. Mala called back to let us know that Rocky Mountain Helicopters and Anchorage's Providence Hospital medevac team were working together to bring the Russian boy to Texas, for free. He and the boy would arrive in twenty-six hours.

The boy's name was Anton Avdeyenko. The afternoon he arrived, the local news media interviewed me—this was big news, because it was the first time anyone had been permitted to leave the Soviet Union to receive medical treatment. The press asked the usual questions: what happened to Anton, what would the surgeries entail, what were his prospects for full recovery, etc.

"Anton has one of the deepest burns I've ever seen," I told them. "He's been burned over thirty-three percent of his body. In Magadan, the wounds had become extensively infected with bacteria, and they've now reached down to muscle and bone. We've already started administering massive doses of antibiotics, and because too much of his own skin was burned, we will surgically treat his wounds with cadaver skin."

It was the first of several such interviews, and they all went well. I was comfortable on camera, and many said I was a natural.

In the coming weeks, Anton began to heal wonderfully. Our surgeries were successful, and soon we made plans to send Anton back to Magadan. When the press interviewed the boy through a translator, he said, "The happiest moment was that I got back up on my feet, and that I came out alive. The doctors who treated me in Texas were the best of all."

Seeing an overjoyed patient was always the greatest reward of being a burn surgeon.

During that time, my secretary, Monica, buzzed my office one afternoon to tell me that 911 was on the phone and wanted to talk to me. I had a great deal of respect for the emergency medical service, and I wondered what sort of advice they might be seeking from me. Perhaps they wanted to discuss what type of resuscitation fluids they should carry on their ambulances, or maybe what type of splints. I picked up the phone, quite pleased they would call me.

The woman on the other end of the phone started asking questions having to do with filming, something about a TV show and Russians. I must have sounded confused, because Monica finally came in and whispered that "911" was a television show. Ah. A network television show wanted to do a story about Anton. I told them it was fine with me as long as Anton and his mother gave permission. I checked with them and they did.

Later that day, I was in my office proofing operative reports when Monica buzzed my office.

Monica: Dr. Waymack, the 911 people want to know if you'd like
            to play yourself in the show.
Me: Uh, no. Tell them thanks but no thanks. I've got patients
            to take care of.

A couple of weeks later, "the 911 people" called to say they would be arriving in town on Tuesday, and could they please interview me that afternoon. They would film the scenes for the show the following day.

"Well, okay," I told Monica. "I guess I can answer a few questions."

As luck would have it, the night before they arrived there was a car crash, and I spent most of the night in the operating room. I got about an hour of sleep, so I was quite tired Tuesday, and still had a full day's work ahead of me.

By the time the television crew arrived late that afternoon, I was exhausted. The 911 crew brought TV cameras, sound equipment, and all sorts of other gadgets into my office. The set designer breezed in and promptly said, "No, no, no, this won't do, his furniture is all out of position," so the crew removed all the equipment, rearranged my office furniture, then brought all their stuff back. Meanwhile, I tried valiantly to stay awake.

Once the set designer was satisfied with my office, the director took about ten minutes off-camera to ask me some questions about Anton. I answered them the same way I had always answered reporters' questions: calm, articulate, decisive. The director was pleased and said I would be just great on camera.

"This won't take too long," he said reassuringly.

Since my major desire was now to get home and hibernate for twelve hours, I was pleased to hear this. I smiled as they turned on the bright camera lights. Showtime!

"Okay, Doc, now I'm going to ask you the same questions, but this time on tape, ok?" the director said. "You'll do great. Just pretend I'm not here when you answer the questions. Just act like you're all alone. They'll edit my voice out later."

The problem with this well-intentioned direction was that, in my sleep-deprived state, I actually did act like I was the only room in the room. For two hours. While I struggled to stay awake.

When I was a third-year med student on the psychiatry rotation, I regularly interviewed schizophrenics in an office, just the two of us. At first they seemed aware that I was in the room. But as the interview went on, and their answers grew in duration, the patients seemed to forget that I was there. They would start talking to the walls, to the ceilings, and to nonexistent people. Their eyes roamed the room as they spoke, never focusing on anything, much less me. It was all very eerie.

I am sure by the time my interminable shoot was over, the crew of 911 must have had that same feeling. To pretend I was alone, I told myself not to focus my eyes on anyone in the room, especially not the camera. Thus my eyes meandered about the room, because if I looked at anything for more than a couple of seconds, it would come into focus.

Compounding the problem, I used the same tone of voice that I use when I'm talking to myself. In an interview with a reporter, when I'm engaged in a back-and-forth conversation, I frequently change the tone and amplitude of my voice. When I talk to *myself*, however, my voice comes out monotone and subdued. So for two hours, I talked in a voice guaranteed to put everyone to sleep, while my eyes darted wildly about the room. Undoubtedly the crew of 911 found this action to be every bit as disturbing as I did when I was interviewing schizophrenic patients.

From time to time the director would say "Cut!" with increasing exasperation. At that point, I'd stop pretending I was all alone and talk to him. He'd talk about Anton, I'd talk about Anton. Then he'd say, "*That's* the kind of stuff I want to hear on tape!" The cameraman would begin shooting again, the sound man would start recording again, and I would once more pretend I was all alone in the room. It was like I had gone into a trance.

Not surprisingly, the director managed to get about ten seconds of useful material from the two-hour interview.

I know I should have done what I had always done in television interviews: focus my eyes on the person asking the questions, and change the tone and volume of my voice from time to time. But it's really not my fault. First, I learned to follow orders in the Army. I was now genetically predisposed to take direction from those in charge. Second, having had very little sleep the night before, my brain was not functioning in top form.

Once the shoot was done, the director—with a look of complete hopelessness—told me they had not found anyone to play me in the surgery scenes, and asked, with some hesitation, if I could play myself. The crew groaned. I did too, then went home and collapsed in bed. I strongly suspect the film crew headed to the nearest bar.

The following afternoon at two o'clock, after finishing my surgery in the University of Texas Hospital, I went across the street to the OR in the Shriners Hospital. The film crew had set up shop, and there were cameras and lights everywhere. A child actor had on realistic makeup that made him look like a burn patient, and for the next half hour, my team and I pretended to operate on him. I'm sure the crew must've marveled at my astounding transformation from drug-addled schizophrenic to articulate, engaged surgeon.

Once we finished filming that scene, the crew moved all the equipment to the "recovery room." Since real patients were in the real recovery room, that location was out. Instead, we used a regular patient room. It took some time to set up all the lights and cameras in that room, and I kept telling the director I had to leave at four for a meeting with a patient's family.

At ten to four, they were finally ready to film the next scene. We did one take, but the director scrapped it and ordered a take two. I told him I had to leave, and he and the crew were aghast. They begged me to stay for one more take, but I said the care of my real patients had to come first.

A male nurse happened to pass by the room as I was leaving. A member of the crew grabbed him and told him to pretend he was me for ten minutes.

So, if you happened to catch the episode of Rescue 911 where a burned Russian child was saved in a U.S. hospital, you might have wondered why at one point the American doctor went from being a 6'5" guy with brown hair to a 5'9" guy with red hair. Now you know the answer.

It didn't hurt my feelings that Hollywood never called me back for an encore performance—I far preferred playing a surgeon in real life.

A Final
Promotion

WHEN I LEFT THE ARMY to become an associate professor at the University of Texas, I retained my commission and remained in the Individual Ready Reserve (IRR). Members of the IRR aren't obligated to do monthly drills or annual training; they only need to keep themselves available for active duty if the President calls them up. The Army makes the IRR available for surgeons since the training they would need for war is something they already do on a daily basis: operate on patients.

Two years after I left active duty for the IRR, I received a letter from the Army Medical Command. As soon as I saw the envelope, I thought, *Uh oh. They found out.*

For the entire two and a half years I was in the Army on active duty, no one but Sergeant Marr knew that I had received my commission as a major without having attended the U.S. Army's Officer Candidate School. In fact, I was pretty sure I was the *only* Army officer to have done so. And now the Army had finally noticed.

The letter read:

"Congratulations! You have been promoted to lieutenant colonel."

The letter also stated something to the effect of, "Oh by the way, we don't seem to be able to locate the paperwork certifying that you have completed OCS. Would you please be so kind as to send us a copy of that certificate, or in the highly unlikely event that you never did complete the course, when would you like to spend a few weeks taking it?"

I ignored it. I figured it would take another two and a half years before the Army realized I hadn't sent in the paperwork.

Part VI

The Siberian Surgeon

1989-1991

Call-up Orders
to Siberia

WHEN I ACCEPTED THE ARMY'S OFFER to be chief of surgical studies, part of the deal was that I would be based in San Antonio, Texas. After nine winters in Ohio, I never wanted to deal with cold weather or snow again. For the first two years, being an Army surgeon based in San Antonio seemed like a great idea. Then I got a phone call that changed all that.

It was about eleven o'clock one June night in 1989, and I was sound asleep in my bed when the telephone rang.

"Major Waymack speaking," I said, still groggy.

"Major, do you have your passport readily available?" an officer said.

"Huh? Yeah. Why?"

"Report to base at 0700 hours, and bring civilian clothes and your passport," he said. "You've been ordered to the Soviet Union."

"What?!" I said, half laughing, sitting up. This must be a joke. "Ordered to the Soviet Union by *whom?*"

"By the President of the United States." Click.

The exact sequence of events that led to this phone call involved many people throughout the world. It all started in 1984, when Mikhail Gorbachev—then only a member of the Soviet Politburo—visited Great Britain and met with British Prime Minister Margaret Thatcher.

"I like Mr. Gorbachev," she told the BBC afterward. "We can do business together."

I remember watching coverage of the historic meeting on ABC News' "World News Tonight with Peter Jennings." As I listened to that report, it never occurred to me that I was to be part of the royal "we."

The next month, Prime Minister Thatcher met with President Ronald Reagan at Camp David, and her optimism about Gorbachev strengthened Reagan's own hopefulness about U.S.-Soviet relations. Six months later, Gorbachev took over the Kremlin, aiming to end the Cold War. That November, Reagan invited the Soviet leader to a summit in Geneva, where they got along famously. The three world leaders formed a unique friendship triangle, and the Cold War started to thaw. When George H.W. Bush was elected president in the fall of 1988, he picked up where Reagan left off.

Then on June 4, 1989, a catastrophic accident occurred in the USSR's Ural Mountains. A natural gas pipeline that ran near the tracks of a trans-Siberian railway exploded just as two trains were passing in opposite directions. A colossal fireball erupted, and the flames spread out for more than a mile, enveloping the surrounding forest. Hundreds of trees were instantly incinerated.

The explosion blew out windows ten miles away, and demolished thirty-seven train cars and two locomotives. I have pictures of the aftermath of the devastation, and I can attest that it was truly horrific. Many scientists described the blast as rivaling that of the atomic bomb dropped on Hiroshima.

The two trains were carrying a total of about 1,300 passengers, many of them families traveling to and from summer holidays on the Black Sea. Almost 600 passengers died instantly from the force of the blast, and around 200 died shortly thereafter. Eyewitnesses saw people "burning like matches." Those who survived had severe burn injuries.

Most of the survivors were taken to Ufa, the nearest big city. The Ufa burn hospital had seventy-five beds that filled up very quickly, and the remaining patients were distributed among other hospitals throughout the city.

The physicians and surgeons at the other hospitals had zero burn experience or training. In the Soviet Union, if the state decided you were to be a burn surgeon, you received five years of training after high school to become a physician, then three more years of training as a burn surgeon. Similarly, if the state decided you were to be an intestinal surgeon, you did three years of intestinal surgery after medical school. Individual surgeons in the Soviet Union could only perform a very limited number of types of operations.

In contrast, surgeons in the U.S. can perform all sorts of surgeries, even those outside their specialty. To become a burn surgeon, for example, I completed four years of college, four years of medical school, a five-year general surgery residency during which I studied all types of surgery, and then a one-year burn fellowship during which I only performed burn surgery. In an emergency, I could perform an appendectomy or deliver a baby. Likewise, a heart surgeon in the U.S. could perform burn surgery if no burn surgeon were available.

In Ufa, the only surgeons available who knew anything about treating burns were those in the burn center. Around 500 burn victims desperately needed treatment, but there were only seventy-five beds.

When news of the tragedy spread, President George Bush sent his condolences and offered the Soviets any assistance. Gorbachev gladly took him up on it. In short order, someone from the White House called someone at the Pentagon, who told the White House to call us. Our unit commander got a call about 10:45 p.m. from someone at the White House, who said the President wanted to send an Army burn team to the Soviet Union, to a city on the edge of Siberia.

Since I was the head of one of the burn teams, President Bush was asking *me* to go. I was honored to get a personal call-up from our commander in chief.

On the other hand… sometimes I've wondered if the real reason I was chosen was that, when the Pentagon learned the President wanted to send an Army officer and his team, the Pentagon could think of no one they'd rather send to Siberia than me.

In the hours between that 11:00 p.m. phone call and my 7:00 a.m. arrival on base, I packed my suitcases with civilian clothes, plus all the granola bars, packets of Kleenex, and bottled water I could get from the local 7-11 at 3:00 a.m. My trip to China had taught me well.

We took off from Kelly Air Force Base in a Lockheed C-141 strategic airlifter and made a refueling stop at Andrews Air Force Base, just outside Washington, D.C. We arrived at Ramstein Air Base in southwestern Germany around noon the next day.

By the time we arrived at Ramstein, my team and I were tired and needed a shower and shave. The White House envoy told us we wouldn't be leaving for the Soviet Union for another three hours, so we had some time to kill.

We headed to the only hotel on base, figuring we could rent some rooms and have a quick shower and shave. I asked the middle-aged German woman at the front desk if we could rent rooms for just a couple of hours. She narrowed her eyes and looked at the scruffy bunch of fellows with me.

"You want room for couple hours only?" she asked suspiciously. "How many 'couple'?"

"Um, just, you know, like two hours?" I said. "Maybe three?"

"Three!" she said, aghast. "No, sir. This is respectable hotel. You go off base for that kind of thing!"

"No, no!" I exclaimed. "We just need two rooms for two hours so we can shower and shave. We've been on a long plane flight."

She looked us up and down like she was considering whether we looked like the type of Army soldiers who would smuggle German prostitutes up to the rooms.

"Please?" I said nicely. The rest of my team straightened up and tried to look as respectable as possible.

She still looked very skeptical, so I showed her a copy of our orders.

"We're on our way to the Soviet Union," I explained. "President Bush sent us on a mission."

She relented, and we gratefully took two rooms and got cleaned up.

Soon we were airborne and headed due north to bypass East Germany, since its president refused our request to fly over his country. (This was a few months before the Berlin Wall fell, and the Cold War had not yet ended.) Eventually, after a lengthy series of detours, we landed at Sheremetyevo International Airport in Moscow around midnight.

We had brought 15,000 pounds of medical supplies with us as a gesture of goodwill. Our plan was to transfer the supplies onto a Soviet air transport, and the Russians would then fly us and the supplies on to Ufa, about 1,000 miles east of Moscow.

At the Moscow airport, however, several unsmiling Soviet officials in uniform informed us of a change in plans. Not a single transport plane was available in the entire country, so the Soviet pilots would have to fly the American C-141 on to Ufa. Unsurprisingly, the U.S. Air Force would not authorize the Soviets' plan. After about an hour of high-level negotiations, with input from the Pentagon and the White House, the Soviets grudgingly acquiesced, with one condition: the Americans would fly the C-141 on to Ufa, but a Russian navigator would be in the cockpit to navigate and make sure the plane didn't get lost.

Just in case, you know, we didn't have any maps.

During the three-hour flight to Ufa, I wandered into the cockpit several times. Each time I found the American pilot and copilot flying the plane, while the Soviet "navigator" took endless notes. Now, I'm not a pilot, but even I could recognize that the navigator wasn't taking notations on our position vis-à-vis the stars, but rather the plane's handling and performance capabilities.

I didn't share Mrs. Thatcher's confidence about doing business with the Russians.

Soviet Airports

IN 1989, civilian Soviet airports worked a little differently from airports in the West. If a Soviet official ordered you to go somewhere—and you wouldn't be going anywhere unless the Party ordered you, or at least gave you permission—you would go to the airport and await a flight. Sometimes this meant waiting in the airport lobby for two or three days. Eventually, you would be informed that you had been assigned to the next flight, and instructed to be ready to board.

Before the mid-'90s, Western-style jetways from the terminal to the airplane didn't exist in the Soviet Union. Once your name had been called, you and the other passengers would leave the terminal and walk down the taxiway, climb up the stairs and board the plane. In Ufa, they boarded about ten Aeroflot Soviet Airlines jets at once, early each morning. Thus, shortly after dawn on any given morning, you could expect to see around 2,000 Soviet citizens walking from the Ufa International Airport down the taxiway to their airplanes.

Another interesting thing about the USSR in 1989 is that all Soviet citizens had been taught since the end of WWII that the Americans would one day invade their country. From the time they started school, little Soviet children were indoctrinated with this inevitable certainty.

Thus, when our behemoth U.S. Air Force C-141 descended from the clouds at the very moment some 2,000 Russians were walking down this taxiway, we created quite a stir. The aircraft was decorated with a big American flag on its tail, so there was no doubt about the identity of the invaders.

As soon as we landed and pulled up near the Aeroflot jets, we hopped off the plane. I think it's fair to say that we were just as startled to see a couple of thousand people staring at us in shock as they were to see a group of Americans emerge from the biggest airplane most of them had ever seen.

Apparently—much like my experience in China—only the air traffic controller and the minister and deputy minister of health for the Soviet province of Bashkiria had known we were coming. They in turn only notified three others: a bus driver who would take us to our hotel and two citizens to haul our equipment in a pickup truck.

Boris and Sasha's vehicle was slightly smaller than your average 1960s-era Ford pickup truck. When we disembarked, they drove their little truck to the rear of the C-141 and waited for the pilot to open the cargo doors. I guess they weren't expecting to see 15,000 pounds of equipment in two dozen wooden pallets that were each about the size of their pickup truck.

They resourcefully figured out a new plan, and the equipment eventually made it to the various hospitals. Meanwhile, the bus driver took us to the best hotel in Ufa, where high-ranking party officials stayed when they were in town. We had breakfast as soon as we arrived: hot tea, bread, cheese, and curdled mare's milk. I learned my first four Russian words that day: *chai* (tea), *hliep* (bread), *syr* (cheese), and *bolshe* (more). I decided there was no need to learn how to ask for more curdled mare's milk—one helping was enough for a lifetime.

An Overlooked
Patient

AFTER BREAKFAST, almost everyone on our jet-lagged team went to bed. I was anxious to see the burn victims, though, so I went with two of my colleagues to make rounds at various hospitals. Dr. Bill Becker was another burn surgeon, and Dr. Al McManus was a microbiologist who was in charge of culturing burn wounds to determine the nature of their infection.

Our hosts first took us to the burn hospital for the Bashkir Autonomous Soviet Socialist Republic, which had room for seventy-five patients but was treating ninety. We saw every single patient. Just seeing the quantity of patients was a numbing experience—no city on this planet, not even New York or Los Angeles, could have adequately dealt with 500 burn patients at once. But the sheer overwhelming numbers were compounded by a lack of adequate supplies and properly trained burn surgeons. Burn patients require more intensive care than any other type of patient, and the Russians did not begin to have the resources to supply such care.

Next we went to a cancer hospital filled with burn patients; the victims of the explosion were so numerous they took every empty bed in every hospital in Ufa. The scenario was the same as at the burn hospital. We went from bed to bed, ward to ward, and floor to floor, seeing all the burn patients. For each one, we reviewed the patient's medical history as well as the plan for their future treatments.

Finally, we reached the intensive care unit. One patient was wrapped in bandages from head to toe; the only parts of his body you could see were his mouth and one foot. An endotracheal tube connected to a ventilator was doing the breathing for him. As I listened to the doctor's presentation of this patient's case, I was concerned that the patient wasn't moving, except for the rhythmic rising and falling of his chest. This movement was in perfect synchrony with the ventilator inhaling and exhaling for him— which is unusual because there's always some asymmetry in the movement, due to variations in chest muscle tone.

When a patient's chest moves up and down in perfect symmetry, this generally means he's been given paralyzing drugs. This is occasionally necessary when the patient fights the ventilator—when he struggles against its efforts to breathe for him. When that happens, you first give the patient sedatives to try to relax him, but if that fails and you're still not getting enough oxygen into him, you're compelled to give him drugs that temporarily paralyze him. It's a dangerous move, since if the endotracheal tube were to come out, the patient wouldn't be able to breathe on his own and would suffocate in three minutes.

I assumed the doctors had given this patient a paralyzing drug. I looked up to check the monitor for his pulse and blood pressure, but there was no monitor. In the United States, failure to continually monitor a paralyzed patient on a ventilator would have constituted gross malpractice. In the Soviet Union, however, that was standard operating procedure.

As I continued to carefully study the patient, it occurred to me that the doctors might not be able to tell if the patient were to die. After all, he was on no electrical heart monitor, and the ventilator would continue to pump oxygen into his lungs until someone unplugged it.

He was, in fact, dead. His unbandaged foot was pale, but I glanced underneath and saw what I had missed when I first came in: the heel was a dark blue, evidence that lividity had begun at least eight hours ago. "Lividity" refers to the final stage of death where heavy red blood cells sink to the lower portion of your body. In other words, if you die prostrate, gravity will pull your blood down into the back of your chest, abdomen, arms, legs, and feet, turning them all dark blue within eight to twelve hours.

I didn't want to insult the Soviet doctors by insinuating they couldn't tell a live patient from a very cold dead corpse, so I tried to inconspicuously check for a pulse. As soon as the doctor and translator turned away toward another doctor, I discreetly stretched my fingers toward the dorsalis pedis artery on the patient's foot. The doctor and translator turned back around, and I quickly retracted my hand.

We continued discussing the patient's case, and when they turned away to speak to another doctor, I inched forward and stealthily reached my hand out toward the dark blue foot. Again they turned around just before my fingers could touch the artery. I quickly withdrew my hand.

The scenario repeated itself several times. I should have said something, but my sleep-deprived brain wasn't thinking clearly. Across the patient's bed, an equally tired Al McManus initially stared in confusion at my apparently intermittent seizures, as my hand jerked toward and then away from the patient's foot. He stared down at the foot for a few moments. Then abruptly, his eyes suddenly got rather large.

The Soviet doctors finished their presentations and motioned us to follow them to the next room. Al and I lagged behind them as they walked down the hallway, and as the rest of the team turned around the corner, we did a U-turn and headed back to the ICU. We got to the doorway and saw the remaining doctors and nurses ripping the bandages off the dead patient, looking for signs of life; apparently they too had noted my movements and realized my diagnosis.

I was very sorry about the dead patient, but relieved that I hadn't insulted the Soviets by implying their medical degrees were worthless. In their defense, they didn't lack intelligence, just adequate medical equipment. In that regard, the Soviets were at least thirty years behind the U.S. standard of medical care.

The Horror Show

A S A LONGTIME BURN AND TRAUMA SURGEON, I had become hardened to the point that nothing could bother me. I could sit and eat lunch while watching an autopsy. I could handle multiple car-crash victims in the ER without stressing. I could use a machine to suck brains leaking from a patient's fractured skull into his nose so I could thread a breathing tube down the nose into the lungs. If I realized a situation was hopeless, I would move on to the next patient without giving it a moment's thought.

About the only thing that still bothered me were child-abuse cases. But that first day in Ufa, I found myself quite emotionally affected. It's not that the Russian patients had worse burns than those I routinely saw back home—it was the standard of care that depressed me.

I was used to seeing burn patients taken to the operating room, where I cut away their dead burned skin and replaced it with living skin. I was used to seeing burn patients treated with creams that prevented infections, and kept in clean rooms. This wasn't just an American standard of care; I had watched doctors in the interior of China care for their burn patients with these same standards.

But in Ufa, I saw patients kept in rooms that were dirtier than the broom closets in Western hospitals. Burned skin was not surgically cut away but allowed to rot. Soviet surgeons performed skin grafts only after the dead skin had completely rotted away and fallen off the wounds—if the patients were still alive by then. Patients were not treated with the antimicrobial creams I had taken for granted in the United States.

The sheer magnitude of the problem compounded my depression. I saw dozens of burn patients that first day, and the number grew into the hundreds by the second day. Not one was receiving anything close to adequate care by our Western standards. The patients simply laid there on dirty beds in dirty rooms with their dead skin rotting away and becoming increasingly contaminated with bacteria.

The sickening pit in my stomach reminded me of how I felt when I first watched *Gone with the Wind*. There's a scene where Scarlett arrives at the Army hospital, and is taken aback by the wounded soldiers lying on dirty cots in primitive conditions. Then the camera pans out, and you see the few soldiers expand to dozens and then hundreds, all desperately awaiting care in wretched, unsterile conditions.

Seeing such a miserable scene in real life was awful. The patients and their cries of pain were real, the stench of actual rotting flesh permeated the rooms—and I wasn't sure if I would be able to help them. That was the worst part. All of this weighed on me terribly.

Exhausted physically, mentally, and emotionally, I slept for nearly eleven uninterrupted hours that first night. When I woke up at six the next morning, for a moment I hoped it had all been a bad dream. I pulled myself together, got out of bed and showered, and determined to get to work and see what I could do for these hundreds of burn victims.

Downstairs in the dining room, half our team was already having breakfast. I greeted our nurse (an Army captain), two corpsmen (sergeants), and our government-issued translator from Washington, D.C., and told them about my experience the day before. I wanted to prepare them for the shock of what they were about to see.

"But no matter how distressed you become," I warned them, "don't ever tell the Soviet doctors they've done something wrong. Even if you're appalled by their standard of care."

One of the corpsmen looked a little confused.

"But I thought we came to help the doctors," he said. "How can we teach them proper care if we don't point out their mistakes?"

"Well, we just have to be diplomatic about it," I said. "We were sent here not only to help the burn victims but also to improve Soviet-American relations. And we can't do that if we come across as critical or condescending."

They all nodded, understanding.

"What looks incorrect by our standards is just considered routine care here," I continued. "So we have to be culturally sensitive and not offend them by telling them they're doing it wrong. Just encourage them as they learn our techniques. Be positive and supportive."

The team listened, and followed my instructions to the letter. When we saw the Soviet doctors and nurses doing something that would have been considered malpractice in the U.S., we would merely say, "Oh, that's an interesting way of doing that. In America we do it slightly different. It probably works both ways."

Invariably, the Soviets would respond, "Oh. How do *you* do it?"

Then we would show them. While they may have lacked the training and the resources we Americans had, the Soviet doctors were intelligent. They were dedicated physicians doing the best they could with the little they had. They could see that our surgical methods and ways of caring for patients were frequently superior to theirs, and they learned the new techniques and standards quickly.

That morning at breakfast, I gave similar instructions to our translator, who had no background in medicine.

"Things will go horribly wrong," I said frankly, "but I want to keep the Soviet doctors optimistic. So any time they attempt to learn one of our techniques, we're going to tell them, 'Good.'"

The translator nodded in agreement. I sighed, just thinking of the enormous task ahead of us—medically and diplomatically.

"I mean, this might be the biggest horror show in the history of burn wound care," I reiterated, making sure the translator understood what I would be doing. "But even if the Soviet doctors totally screw up, I'll just say, 'Good, good,' and then show them how to do it properly, OK?"

"Got it," he said. "You want to make sure that I say 'good' even when you look alarmed."

"Exactly," I said, nodding. "Now, how do you say 'good' in Russian?

Just so I can recognize what you're saying."

"Horror show," he responded.

"Yes, it probably will be. But how do you say 'good'?" I asked.

"No, that's how you say 'good,'" he answered with a chuckle. "Ho-roh-sho is 'good' in Russian."

Wow. What were the chances?

The Russians were quite pleased to hear us saying *khorosho* whenever they attempted to learn a new technique.

I warned the team about one other thing that morning at breakfast. I had read in *The Wall Street Journal* about a year before that one of the most common causes of burn injury in the Soviet Union was exploding television sets.

"So I'd highly recommend not turning on the TV," I cautioned them.

Everyone laughed.

"Good one, Doc," said one of the corpsmen.

"I'm not kidding," I said. "This is actually a common occurrence."

They didn't believe me for a second.

Two days later, they took my warning seriously. Sergeant Lorsch came down to breakfast on the third morning with a story that corroborated my warning.

At about 3:00 a.m., he had been awakened by what sounded like thunder, followed by a persistent volley of hard, steady rain. He rolled over in bed and was about to fall back asleep when he realized that the thunder and rain were coming from behind his head, not the window. He got up to investigate, and opened the bathroom door. To his dismay, he found that the toilet had exploded, and water was shooting up from a hole in the floor.

There was no telephone in the room, so Lorsch threw on a T-shirt and pants and quickly headed down the hallway to the third-floor desk. In sign language, he motioned for the attending babushka to follow him.

"She wasn't at all surprised when she walked into the bathroom!" Lorsch told us, dumbfounded. "She just walks over to the corner, turns a knob in the wall, and the water stops shooting up."

"What did she say?" our nurse asked.

"I don't know!" he responded, shrugging helplessly. "She said something, but I don't speak Russian!"

After that, the team believed me when I warned them about exploding things. We were also careful to avoid calling bathrooms "restrooms" during our stay, as we certainly never rested in them. We gingerly, tentatively did our business, always ready to make a mad dash for it if we heard any thunder-like sounds. That experience certainly gave "horror show" a whole new meaning.

Soviet
Proctologists

AFTER BREAKFAST, the whole team was loaded onto a bus and taken to Hospital 21, which normally was only for patients with colon and rectal problems. In the aftermath of the railway disaster, however, it was filled with burn victims. The doctors were all proctologists and had had no burn-care experience prior to the explosion.

After we made rounds, the Soviet doctors asked if I would like some tea. While we relaxed for a short break, I told them of my background in burn surgery, and asked if they had any experience in that field.

"*Nyet*," they said almost in unison, shaking their heads. I didn't need the translator for that one.

"Then this is a wonderful opportunity to exchange ideas on burn care!" I said with a smile. I waited for the translator, and they all nodded eagerly.

"So how would an American burn doctor take care of such patients?" asked one of the proctologists.

"Well, we would take them to the operating room as soon as possible and surgically cut away the burn wounds," I explained. "Then we would perform skin grafts."

They shook their heads and looked abashed.

"Unfortunately, we do not have any equipment for doing such operations," one replied.

"Oh, we brought some from the United States!" I said brightly. "It's all for you, free of charge. We have all the instruments you need for burn surgeries."

They were delighted, and asked if I could perform surgeries on three patients the next day, so they could watch and learn.

We arrived the next morning, eager to finally get to work. All the team, that is, except Capt. Andrea Conen, the nurse, who wasn't thrilled about assisting me in surgery.

"I'm an extremely competent ICU nurse," she explained, somewhat defensively, "but I haven't set foot in an OR since nursing school."

"Hmm," I responded, puzzled. "So why were you assigned as my nursing assistant?"

"Because no one thought to include OR nurses on this trip!" Andrea exclaimed, with a look that said *What are you asking ME for? It's not my damn fault!*

Well, I needed a nurse who knew a Kocher clamp from Metzenbaum scissors and could hand me the right hemostat in her sleep. I needed to know I could depend on an assistant, because plenty of other things would likely go wrong. First of all, the electrical surgical equipment we brought used 220 volts, but the Soviet electrical system ran on 110. Using a transformer was going to make me a little nervous. Then there was the Soviet anesthesiologist—probably competent, but he would be difficult to communicate with if something went wrong. And finally, if anything *did* go wrong, it could potentially create a diplomatic incident with global ramifications.

I arrived in the OR and learned that the anesthesiologist planned to use ether. *Ether?* I thought, astonished. *That went out about forty years ago!* It's just too dangerous as an anesthetic—it's got a nasty tendency to explode at inopportune times, like in the middle of an operation.

It's okay, I told myself, trying to calm down. *At least they have something.*

But it got worse from there. I glanced around the OR and could immediately see it wasn't even close to being sterile by Western standards. Operating rooms shouldn't have windows, for example, because outside air is contaminated. The air supply to ORs in the U.S. comes through special air ducts that filter out bacteria. This Soviet operating room not only had windows—they were open. And I counted at least five flies that flew in while I was staring in disbelief. I tried to conceal my dismay, because twenty-seven Soviet doctors were watching me.

Then I found out that the blood we would be giving the patient had not undergone a cross-match test. I had no idea how we were going to pull off this surgery without killing the patient. I found myself actually yearning to be back in that VA Hospital OR on that day the lights went out.

Surprisingly, though, things went quite smoothly. Whenever I needed an instrument, I would point to it and say, "Captain, why don't you hand me that hemostat?" Andrea was smart and learned quickly, and anyway, the Soviet doctors were too busy admiring her to notice when she made a mistake.

After a couple of hours of hard work, and by the grace of God, we successfully completed the operation. We had replaced all the burn wounds with normal skin. Andrea and I were about to collapse onto the stools in the corner, but the Soviet doctors were so delighted by our performance that they all wanted to take turns giving us huge Russian bear hugs and kisses on both cheeks. I was pleased that they were so enthusiastic and in awe of my skill as a burn surgeon. It occurred to me later, however, that perhaps they were just enthusiastic about hugging and kissing the attractive Army captain.

We then moved on to the next OR, where the anesthesiologist had just finished sedating another burn patient. I motioned to one of the Soviet surgeons to scrub in and assist us.

In med school, the learning model is "see one, do one, teach one." After a doctor has witnessed a procedure for the first time, he should be assisted in doing the next one, and then teach someone else how to do it. I believe in that model, within reasonable guidelines. As soon as the Soviet doctor had finished scrubbing his hands and donning the OR gown and gloves, I handed him the dermatome—the electric knife used to cut away dead burned skin and to harvest living skin. Instantly, he realized that I wanted him to do this case, and his eyes lit up like a kid on Christmas morning.

A couple of hours later, another burn patient had been successfully excised and skin grafted, and another round of hugging and kissing followed. It seemed to me that Andrea got more than her fair share of the congratulatory affection.

The third case went as well as the first two, and another Soviet surgeon had now performed Western-style burn surgery. Once the day's operations were over, the twenty-five remaining surgeons all clamored to make ward rounds and find more patients to operate on. They were all eager to have their own turn.

Of course, I didn't need three medical degrees to figure out basic male psychology: I'm sure the Soviets were just as motivated by the reward of hugging and kissing an attractive Army nurse as they were by the opportunity to try a new technique. It was actually comforting to find common ground with our Soviet comrades—perhaps we were more alike than we were different.

Un-disposable Surgical Gowns

B EFORE AN OPERATION CAN BEGIN, everyone in the OR must put on a surgical gown over their scrubs. For decades, this gown was made of cotton fabric so tightly knit that bacteria from the surgeons and nurses couldn't infect the patient. The surgeon would scrub the patient with antimicrobial soap, then place tightly woven cotton drapes on the patient, covering every inch except for the area of operation. After surgery, the gowns and drapes were thoroughly washed in the hospital laundry, then sterilized in an autoclave, which heated them under pressure to nearly 200°F.

In the late '70s, medical-device companies in the U.S. developed surgical drapes and gowns made of paper. Not only did they decrease the rate of infections in surgical patients, they were also disposable. By the mid-1980s, paper gowns and drapes replaced cotton ones as the standard of care in the U.S. and the rest of the developed world—except the Soviet Union.

Included in our 15,000 pounds of equipment were hundreds of paper gowns and paper surgical drapes for our Soviet colleagues. At the end of our first operation in Ufa, we threw the gowns and drapes into the trash. The Soviet head nurse quickly retrieved them and placed them into the "used" bin.

We told the American translator to explain that these were made of paper and thus disposable. The translator said there was no Russian word for disposable (understandably), but told her they were just paper. The nurse frowned and shook her head.

"You cannot take these out of the bin," she said in Russian. "You must wash and re-use them."

Our translator explained again that they were to be thrown away. The head nurse argued with him and waved her finger back and forth in the universal sign language for "no."

I took the gowns out of the cloth bin anyway, and put them in the trash.

"*Nyet!*" she said firmly, glaring at me and pulling them out of the trash. "They belong here in the bin!"

The translator tried explaining one more time. The nurse picked up the cloth bin protectively.

"They go to the laundry room," she said, not budging. "They will be washed by the Soviet laundry personnel and then sent up here for tomorrow's operations."

"You can't wash these," the translator insisted. "They are made of *paper!*"

We gave up. I wasn't going to argue with her—she was bigger than I was and could've taken me in a fistfight.

The nurse sent the paper gowns and drapes we had used for all three operations down to the laundry room, along with instructions to wash them immediately so they would be ready for the next day's operations. The laundry personnel dutifully put them in the laundry machine, added soap, and turned it on. A little over half an hour later, the woman opened the lid and found what could best be described as paper mâché.

Filled with shame, the woman informed the head nurse that all the valuable American gowns and drapes had been destroyed. The nurse was equal parts horrified and livid. The next day the silly tug of war with the paper gowns and drapes repeated, and again we gave up arguing. This time, however, the head nurse went down to supervise the incompetent laundry woman. Fortunately for the humiliated worker, the paper mâché fiasco occurred again, and she thus avoided a sentence of hard labor in Siberia.

The next day, the head nurse once again—although with less conviction—attempted to remove the paper gowns and drapes from the trash. Fed up with the recurring fiasco, I took one of the paper gowns out of the head nurse's hands, and tore it in half with a single pull. The Soviets looked astonished, as though I had super-human strength.

"Disposable!" I said, pointing to the two halves of my gown.

Andrea then took one from the head nurse and ripped it in half as easily as if she had ripped a tissue.

"Disposable!" she said.

Apparently, the concept finally sunk in, and the head nurse never again tried to remove our gowns and drapes from the trash bin. What the Soviets did with the hundreds we left them, however, is anyone's guess.

Vladimir
the Intern

OUR TEAM DIDN'T JUST PERFORM SURGERIES. That first week in Ufa, I ordered a chest X-ray for one of the burn victims, and expected it to come back up by the time I had finished one operation. When it didn't, I asked a Soviet intern to help me out. He had always been with the doctors who watched the operations, and he looked to be about thirty years old, so I assumed he must be a rather senior intern.

"Vladimir," I said, beckoning him over. "Let's go down to the radiology department and see what that X-ray showed."

"Excellent suggestion," Vladimir said. "I will go be informed where radiology department is located."

An intern who didn't know his way around the small hospital? He must've been here for at least a year. *Hmmm...* I thought to myself. *How strange!* Then it clicked.

Vladimir must be a KGB agent.

We talked it over as a team that night at dinner, and decided to have a little fun with him.

For the next few days, whenever one of us saw Vladimir, we would solicit his advice on complex medical issues regarding various patients' conditions.

"Vladimir, do you think this patient is hypotensive?" I asked him casually the next morning.

He thought for a few seconds, then cleared his throat before responding. "I think yes?" he said uncertainly.

"I agree with you," I said. "How did you determine that?"

He looked pensive and scratched his chin.

"I will answer, doctor, as soon as I finish report on previous patient!" he exclaimed, then quickly walked down the hallway.

Later that day, another doctor on the team had a question.

"Vladimir, you're going to be a fine doctor, so I'd love your thoughts," he said. "Which type of bacteria do you think is colonizing this patient's wounds?"

He pondered the question thoughtfully as he looked up at the ceiling.

"Well of course there are many factors that could determine which type bacteria are colonizing wounds," he responded. "That is why Communist Party emphasize good and thorough training and good hygiene. I assume it is same in United States, which types of bacteria colonize. I believe many factors exist that could be quite important."

He looked at the clock.

"I apologize, doctor," he said, "but I must go to meeting with other interns now! We will talk later, yes?"

Another colleague took Vladimir's elbow after the next operation.

"Comrade, what would be a normal white blood cell count for a burn patient in this hospital? Do you think this patient might be developing pre-renal azotemia?"

Vladimir looked blank.

"I… I think I did not study that topic well in our medical university," he said hesitantly. "Maybe when I become attending doctor I know more!"

After a couple of days of this abuse, Vladimir began to avoid us whenever possible. He knew we had identified him as KGB, but he wasn't allowed to admit it to us. When he saw us, he would cringe and begin retreating to the nearest stairwell.

I am sure that each night when he gave a report to his superiors, he must have begged them to not send him back for another day of ridicule. Finally, Vladimir just stopped showing up. I assume the party leaders in Ufa realized he was not obtaining any useful information—or maybe they just took pity on him. We were glad to do our part in creating compassionate communists.

The Battle
of the Banya

AFTER ABOUT A WEEK IN UFA, the Soviets seemed to take a particular liking to me. While the rest of our burn team went back to the hotel for lunch, they started asking me to stay at the hospital and dine with the doctors, hospital administrators, health department officials, and so on. One evening, I got some special treatment I hadn't bargained on.

We were walking from the hospital to our bus, ready for dinner and a well-deserved night's rest, when a black sedan pulled up beside me.

"Please get in car," a man said, opening up the back door from inside. He didn't sound like the invitation was optional, and I was a little nervous about complying.

Our translator, who had been walking next to me, said something to the driver in Russian, who said something back.

"It's okay," the translator said. "You're going to a *dacha.*"

I had no idea what that was, but my orders were to be cooperative with our Russian hosts.

"Um, okay," I said hesitantly, getting into the car. A few seconds later, Andrea slid in next to me.

"Where are we going?" she whispered.

"Hell if I know!" I whispered back.

We didn't need to whisper, since the two men in front apparently didn't know more English than "please get in car." We drove for two hours mostly in silence, and at dusk we arrived at a place that seemed right out of *Doctor Zhivago*. A group of cottages dotted lush green fields and hills, and the Ural Mountains lay in the distance.

The car pulled up in front of one of the cottages, and our Soviet hosts escorted Andrea and me inside. A dozen people were drinking vodka and laughing loudly.

"American doctors!" one of the Soviet surgeons cried when he saw us. "Come! Come!"

The rest of the group erupted with cheers and raised their glasses in a boisterous toast.

The surgeon greeted me with a giant bear hug and a loud kiss on the cheek, and another man happily handed me a large glass of vodka. I noticed that three men were attempting to hug Andrea at the same time. She politely passed on the vodka.

"I'll have hers," I said, and the rowdy group broke out laughing again. Several clapped me on the back.

"A fine comrade!" one exclaimed.

"Perhaps you stay in Soviet Union, yes?" another bellowed. "Our vodka is as fine as your women!"

Andrea smiled gamely at me. I'm sure she was biting her tongue out of diplomatic considerations.

I'm taking one for the team, her look said. *You owe me.*

Some time later, having consumed several liters of vodka between us, one of the men motioned for me to follow him outside.

"*Banya!*" Ivan said, pointing to a small structure behind the cottage.

"Ah!" I responded, nodding. "Bathroom! Thank you!"

Ivan, Sergi, and Igor accompanied me, which I thought was a little odd.

"It's okay, guys," I said. "I've got this."

They escorted me anyway, and when I opened the door I immediately started perspiring. I had entered the outer room of a sauna, and the temperature must've been about 170 degrees.

"*Banya!*" Sergi said. "Take clothes off now!"

I wanted as few clothes on as possible in the oppressive heat, so I didn't argue. I'm not sure why the Soviets thought I would want to sweat more than I already had in a summer heat wave without air conditioning, but it was not my place to question or complain. Once I was naked, they pushed me into the sauna, where I sat down and tried to think cool thoughts. The coldest thing I could imagine was what this region probably had in the winter: a biting Arctic wind blowing -20°F temperatures through cracks in the walls.

While I dreamed of a blizzard, perspiration dripped from every pore. I tried inhaling slowly and deeply, but even breathing in that heat was painful. Then abruptly I gasped as flames seemed to burn my bare back. I glanced over my shoulder in horror and saw the three Russians, each with a large birch branch in their hands, flailing away at my back. Each whipstroke brought a stinging pain to skin already reddened from the heat.

My brain attempted to concentrate through the vodka-induced clouding of my mental processes.

Why are they beating me? I thought frantically. *Do they want information? Should I give them the formula to the burn cream?*

If they wanted the location of our ICBMs, or the blue prints to our stealth bomber, they were going to be sadly disappointed.

"You're torturing the wrong guy!" I shouted, trying to get away from them. "I know nothing!"

Convinced that Vladimir was behind this, I determined to not go down without a fight. I spotted a birch branch over in a corner and made a lunge for it. I grabbed the branch, spun around, and began wildly thrashing it at the three Russians.

To my relief, they retreated. Just in case they tried to attack again, I crouched low in a defensive position and swung the branch in a wide half-circle, back and forth. The men burst out laughing, and I realized I had unwittingly participated in some strange Russian variation of a pillow fight. I nervously laughed along with them, but kept the branch in my hands. The battle may have ended in a tactical draw, but I still consider my sole military encounter of the Cold War a strategic victory.

We finally left the sauna room for the outer room, where we doused ourselves with buckets of cold water. Returning to the main house, we played a game of Russian "pool," which was similar in concept to American pool, but completely different in the execution.

It turned out that playing billiards was considered bourgeois and a capitalist plot to destroy the work ethic of the Russian people, but a high-ranking local party official fell in love with the game while assigned to an overseas post. Before returning to the Soviet Union, he took measurements of a pool table and bought a set of balls and cues. Back in Ufa, he gave the measurements to a local carpenter and had him create the table. Unfortunately, the party official had failed to measure the width of the pockets, so the carpenter had to make an educated guess… and underestimated.

Consequently, we hit dozens of shots that never went into the narrow pockets. After half an hour, I led by the large score of three to two; the final two Soviet players were too drunk to be able to hold a cue and play. (Not so drunk, of course, that they couldn't down more vodka.) We finally graduated to dinner, which consisted of animals shot in the nearby woods: deer, elk, bear, and wild boar. Everything was delicious.

Around 11:00 p.m., our chauffeurs drove Andrea and me back to our hotel in Ufa. The sun had just barely reached the horizon when we left; Siberia was so close to the Arctic Circle that it never got dark in the summer. Around midnight, the sun began to rise again, and it was bright as morning when we got back to the hotel around one. The extraordinary sunrise was a fitting end to a most unusual evening.

Flambé
in the OR

WE USED SOVIET ANESTHESIOLOGISTS during the first two weeks of operations in Ufa, but soon a U.S. Army anesthesiologist flew in to join our team. His arrival—along with his anesthesia machine—was a major relief to me. Not only could I now communicate with the operations anesthesiologist at all times, I also could operate without ether gas in the room.

Since the 1950s, surgery patients in the U.S. have received anesthesia through a tube inserted into their airway. The anesthesia gas is pumped into their lungs with each breath, and when the patient exhales, the gas comes out their lungs and is caught by a trapping device. The advantage of this method is that the OR does not fill up with gas. Moreover, U.S. anesthesiologists use inhalation agents such as ethane, which are not explosive.

In 1980s Soviet Union, however, anesthesiologists exclusively used ether gas anesthesia. Either they put a mask over the patient's face and dripped ether onto it, or they pumped ether in through a breathing tube, but there was no trapping device to catch the gas when the patient exhaled. Thus, by the end of each operation, a lot of ether gas was floating around in the air, and everyone in the OR—not just the patient, but also Capt. Conen, the Soviets, and I—was breathing it in. By the end of each day, I was a little high from ether gas, even though the Soviets had open windows in their ORs to ostensibly prevent this effect.

There were other negative consequences as well.

One day while we were still using a Soviet anesthesiologist, I accidentally dropped a hemostat on the floor during an operation. In the U.S., this wouldn't have been a problem, since surgeons have dozens of hemostats on their instrument trays. However, in the OR in Ufa that day, I only had three. Thus, I needed the hemostat "flashed," or re-sterilized quickly. (Since the usual two-hour sterilization process in an autoclave takes too long, a contaminated instrument needed in surgery can be sterilized in three minutes by heating it up to 200°F with high humidity and pressure.)

The Soviet nurse in charge of the instrument tray picked up the hemostat and walked toward the OR door. I looked up in surprise when I heard a metallic ping, and realized she had dropped it into a metal basin. She grabbed a container of alcohol and poured it over the hemostat. I was about to say "alcohol isn't an adequate disinfectant" when she took out a box of matches, lit one, and dropped it into the basin.

This hemostat flambé was occurring in an OR full of ether gas, so naturally I cringed, waiting for the operating room to explode. Fortunately, it didn't. By the end of the operation, I was still a little shell-shocked by the nurse's recklessness. I considered asking her what the hell she was thinking, but then it occurred to me that perhaps that was standard operating procedure. I took off my gloves and mask and motioned one of the Soviet surgeons over.

"Is that how you always flash-sterilize instruments?" I asked him.

"Of course," he said, looking at me in confusion. "How else would you do it?"

The next day I asked the Pentagon's photographer to come with me to surgery.

"I'm going to drop an instrument on the floor, and I want you to take pictures of how the nurse sterilizes it," I told him.

"Okay, sure," he said. "That doesn't sound very interesting, though."

"You never know," I responded. "It might be."

He followed me into the OR, and during surgery I "accidently" dropped a hemostat on the floor. The photographer snapped away while the nurse picked up the instrument, walked over to the basin, dropped it in, and doused it with alcohol. Just as she dropped the lit match into the basin, he pulled the shutter one last time.

The photographer jumped and let out some nasty words, no translation necessary. He was not at all pleased with me. However, I now have a slightly blurry photograph of what a hemostat flambé looks like in the OR.

A Fly on the (Intestinal) Wall

T HE SOVIET METHOD OF DISPELLING ETHER in the OR was to open all the windows. Of course, an open window not only allows things out, it also allows things in, which is why ORs should have an air filtration system instead.

One day in Ufa, I was taking out a patient's colon. Things were going fine, except for the limited number of instruments and the ether vapors pervading the OR. Fortunately, there was a nice breeze outside, and the ether began to dissipate. I was just about to begin removing part of the patient's colon when something caught my eye. I shifted my gaze, and my eyebrows went up a centimeter.

A garden-variety fly had simply flown in the window and come to rest on the patient's small intestine. It appeared to be drinking the moist serous fluid that coated the outside of the small intestine.

Instinctively, I wanted to do what you usually do when you see a fly: swat it. But it only took me a second to squash that thought, so to speak. You can't obliterate an insect inside a patient's open abdomen—it would likely result in a serious infection. On the other hand, I couldn't let the fly continue to hang out on the patient's small intestine. If the fly were to defecate into the patient's open abdomen, the resulting infection could be fatal.

Despite all my years of training, I was never taught how to remove an insect from the surface of a patient's small intestine in a sterile manner. I therefore improvised. I first tried to nudge the fly with a hemostat, but it just moved an inch south. I wanted to blow it off, but I was wearing a surgical mask. Finally, I took a needle from the tray and poked the fly with it. That worked.

"How'd that colon surgery go?" one of my colleagues asked later.

"Pretty well," I answered. "I had to perform an emergency intestinal procedure I'd never done before, but luckily it worked out."

Gravity Surgery

ONE MORNING AFTER I'D FINISHED a couple of operations, one of the other Army surgeons, Bill Becker, called me to the intensive care unit. I quickly walked down to the dirty and primitive ICU and found Bill standing next to a seriously ill burn patient. "What the hell?" I exclaimed.

The patient was connected to a very primitive apparatus. Two large femoral vein cannulae (small intravenous tubes) were attached to larger pieces of tubing. One of those tubes entered a roller pump, which pulled blood out of that femoral vein and pushed it further along the tubing. The tubing disappeared into a large metal bucket. A second piece of tubing exited the bucket, came back to the patient, and was attached to the other femoral vein cannula. Thus, this contraption pulled blood out of one of the patient's femoral veins, through the tubing into the bucket, then returned the blood through the other end of the tubing into the patient's other femoral vein.

I couldn't see what was inside the bucket into which the two ends of the tubing disappeared, but I thought I could guess. During the early days of kidney dialysis—in the late 1940s and early '50s—doctors would use cannulae to remove blood from patients this way, then pass it through a cylindrical membrane that was somewhat permeable to water and electrolytes. The membrane would be placed in a large container of fluid (the dialysate), and over time the various substances in the blood would dialyze through the membrane into the dialysate. It was a very inefficient and dangerous process for dialysis, but back then, it was all we had.

I assumed this patient had gone into kidney failure and that he was now being dialyzed by a very primitive apparatus. When I looked inside the bucket, however, to my horror I found what was obviously a large animal's spleen. The tubing carrying blood from the patient was being pumped into the spleen's artery. The other end of the tubing was connected to the spleen's vein and was carrying blood back to the patient's other femoral vein.

I stood there for some time trying to comprehend what I was seeing. I looked at Bill with an expression that unmistakably conveyed, *What the f#*% is this?!* Words failed him too—he could only shrug his shoulders and shake his head in amazement.

The head of the ICU saw us standing there, speechless, and walked over.

"This is gravity surgery," he explained proudly, interpreting our stunned looks to mean we were in awe.

I finally found my voice.

"Tell me about it," I said. "What does it do?"

He smiled, happy to teach something to the American surgeons.

"Burn patients' immune systems are very suppressed," he began.

"Yes, I think I've read something about that," I commented, nodding my head. Actually, I had published a number of papers on the subject.

"Spleens are full of white blood cells," he continued lecturing. "So we take patients' suppressed blood and expose to pig's white blood cells to stimulate immune systems."

I nodded thoughtfully, considering my words carefully.

"How well does it work?" I asked.

"Very well," the ICU director responded. "It keeps patients alive for about one day."

"What happens to the control group?" asked Bill.

"Control group?" the director asked. "What is that?"

"That's the group that doesn't get this therapy," Bill answered.

"Why would I deny such great therapy to any patient?" asked the director, perplexed.

Bill and I didn't say anything for a minute.

"I'm curious, doctor," I finally said. "How did you get the idea for this?"

"From the work of German surgeon Eugen Faist," he said proudly.

I just about choked. I personally knew Eugen Faist—he was one of the world's premiere surgical immunologists. Every three years he hosted a huge surgical immunology conference in his hometown of Munich and always invited me to give a few lectures. Eugen had written on how burns and other trauma suppresses the immune system, but I knew that he had never recommended, or even considered, hooking a burn patient up to a pig's spleen in order to stimulate the patient's immune system. The idea was not only ludicrous but dangerous.

"Where do you get the spleens?" I asked casually.

"Oh, local butcher shop," the director answered. "They are not expensive."

"Can we send our photographer to take pictures?" Bill asked.

"Certainly!"

The next morning, our photographer accompanied Igor, the "spleen obtainer," on his trip to the butcher shop. Dozens of dead pigs hung from hooks bolted into the ceiling. The photographer took pictures of the hanging pigs and of Igor slicing open the pig and ripping out the spleen. Nothing, of course, had been sterilized: not the pig's skin, nor the instruments, nor the bucket into which he dropped the spleen.

As if things couldn't get any more horrifying, Igor took the bucket containing the spleen and placed it in the trunk of his car. While he and our photographer stopped for lunch on the way to the hospital, the spleen started cooking in the 100-degree trunk. In the ICU, the director cannulated the femoral veins of some poor patient, then connected the cannulae to the tubing and the tubing to the spleen's artery and vein. The following day, the patient's condition took an irreversible turn for the worse.

Bill and I did try to make the ICU director understand that it was a dangerous procedure, but he brushed us off. We could have argued more vigorously, but we were convinced he wouldn't have listened, and all we would have accomplished was to defeat the main purpose of our mission: to improve Soviet-American relations. So we gave up.

Two years later in Munich, with Eugen and hundreds of other people in the audience, I described the immune-stimulation procedure that surgeons routinely performed in the Soviet Union. My presentation included pictures of the entire system, and I heard audible gasps from the audience. When I finally admitted that the Soviets described Eugen Faist as the "god-father" of this procedure, Eugen was horrified.

Throughout the rest of the conference, one of the world's greatest clinical immunologists had to keep insisting, "I know nothing about that procedure!"

We Only
Take Cash

OUR MISSION ACHIEVED EVERYTHING President Bush could have hoped for, and then some. When we arrived in Ufa, the Soviet doctors predicted we would save only half of our burn patients. By the end of our mission, all eighty of the patients I helped care for survived and went home. I also left behind four Soviet proctologists who were now the best-trained burn surgeons not only in Ufa but in the province of Bashkiria—and quite possibly in all the Soviet Union.

As a token of their gratitude, the Soviets offered the whole team a three-day paid vacation in Moscow on our way home. Everyone accepted but me. As tempting as it sounded—I envisioned being whipped daily in a sweltering *banya*—I wanted to get back to my research lab. As soon as we arrived at the domestic airport in Moscow, I said my farewell to the rest of the team and took a limo to Sheremetyevo International Airport.

The U.S.S.R. deputy minister of health accompanied me.

"My country is most grateful to you Americans," he said through the translator sitting between us.

"It's been an honor to help the Soviet people," I responded with a smile.

"We are indebted to you for your service," he said solemnly.

"No, really, it's been a pleasure to assist your surgeons," I said graciously.

The limo came to a stop at the airport, and the minister pulled something out of his pocket.

"Here is your ticket to New York," he said, handing it to me.

"Thank you!" I said, taking it. "Very kind of you."

The minister kept his hand out, palm up, like he was expecting a tip. "I need 1,500 U.S. dollars, please."

Ah.

I had brought an emergency fund of $2,000 to the Soviet Union, even though I knew our hosts in Ufa would cover the cost of hotels, food, and transportation during our stay. (I brought cash on the assumption that businesses in Siberia weren't accepting American Express just yet.) In fact, the only thing I paid for during our month-long stay was a banquet for the Soviets the night before we left. That cost about $500, so I had just over $1,500 in my wallet.

"Um," I said. "Darn, I only have a thousand on me. Do you take American Express?"

"No," he said. "I can take cash only."

"Hmm," I responded. "Will you take a check?"

The minister looked confused.

"Check?" he asked quizzically. "What is 'check'?"

I explained that it was a piece of paper from a bank and worked just like cash. He looked at me suspiciously, like I was trying to pull a fast one.

"Okay, how about you just keep the ticket and I'll buy a new one inside with my credit card," I said, a little impatiently.

The minister shook his head stubbornly.

"*Nyet.*"

After a prolonged period of negotiation, he finally agreed to take $1,000 in cash and a check for $500. Relieved to have that over with, I got out of the limo and headed inside. We landed in New York, and then I took another flight to San Antonio (happily, that was prepaid). When I finally made it back to Texas, I was so happy to be home that I promptly collapsed on my bed and slept for ten hours.

A few days later, once I'd gotten over jet lag, I completed my government reimbursement forms. I listed $1,500 for the airplane ticket, $500 for the banquet I hosted (an authorized expense), and $20 for the taxi ride home from the airport. A month later, I got a check from the Army for

$1,520. I immediately got on the phone to the reimbursement office and asked about the missing $500.

The officer was curt.

"Major, we don't pay for U.S. Army officers to entertain commies," he said icily.

"The State Department approved it!" I retorted, taken aback. "This was a goodwill humanitarian mission, and we were reciprocating for a banquet our hosts had given us."

"Listen, Major, even if you did get the permission you claimed you got, that was from the State Department," the officer said brusquely. "In case you haven't noticed, you work for the Department of Defense, and our enemy is the Soviet Union. If you want to wine and dine those commies, you'll have to do so at your own expense."

I couldn't change his mind, and I couldn't appeal his decision. The buck stopped with the reimbursement office. I was dismayed when I hung up the phone. In the 1980s, $500 was a lot of money—and the Army didn't pay its surgeons very much.

A week or so later, my bank statement arrived. Not surprisingly, the $500 check to the Soviet government hadn't yet cleared. I assumed it would take a few weeks.

On the following month's statement, however, the check still hadn't cleared... nor did it the next month. In fact, it was never cashed. I can only assume that the deputy minister figured it was worthless and threw it away. I shook my head and laughed. That bizarre exchange at the airport seemed entirely compatible with the rest of my Soviet adventures.

A Midnight Walk
in Moscow

I N THE MONTHS AND YEARS AFTER I RETURNED HOME, my Soviet friends and I exchanged many letters. The four proctologists wrote to me about their careers that had suddenly jumped forward: within six months of my leaving, one of the proctologists had become associate dean of the medical school in Ufa, one had become chief of staff at the cancer hospital in Ufa, and one had become the new chairman of surgery at Hospital 21. Being associated with me was a "career booster," they said.

In fact, the Soviets considered all of us heroes—the entire U.S. Army burn team. A few months after our mission ended, they asked for three of us to come back to Ufa to review the railway accident and the aftermath. They also asked us to stay in Moscow for a few days before continuing on to Ufa, so we could visit the local burn units and the famed Vishnevsky Institute of Surgery.

My colleagues and I landed in Moscow in the middle of winter, and it was bleak, gray, and fiercely cold. As you can imagine, a nine-hour overnight flight from New York to Moscow is rather uncomfortable for a tall guy sitting in coach with his knees to his chest, so I didn't get much sleep. I figured I would fall asleep immediately that night, but at 11:00 p.m I was still wide awake, staring at the ceiling of my hotel room. Although it was pitch black outside, my body thought it was two o'clock in the afternoon.

I finally got up and decided to take a brisk walk around the neighborhood, even though it was snowing. I noticed, unconcerned, that two men followed behind me as I walked down the otherwise empty street toward the bridge over the Moscow River.

I never worried about my personal safety during my trips to the Soviet Union. Almost all Soviets were law-abiding citizens; anyone caught breaking the law was swiftly and harshly punished without the benefit of a real trial. Also, just as in China, I always had "bodyguards" around. KGB agents permanently followed me on all my stays in the Soviet Union, which wasn't surprising since I was a U.S. Army officer.

But while I wasn't worried about my safety, I guess it might have looked strange to be out walking around Moscow in a blizzard around midnight. After all, in 1989 there was no reason to go out after dark in the Soviet Union, especially in the winter. The sparsely stocked stores were all closed, the restaurants were poor quality, and the movies were lousy. On this very cold, windy, and snowy night, the only people in sight were the two men about a hundred yards behind me. Physically and mentally exhausted, I was only vaguely aware of them; I assumed they were out taking a walk, just like me.

When I reached the midpoint of the bridge, I stopped and took in the beautiful scenery. Beneath me was the frozen Moscow River. In the distance, the illuminated Kremlin stood out strikingly against the night sky. And all around me, snow was falling.

I stood there for some time, reflecting on what a strange turn of events my life had taken. If it hadn't been for that student who slipped into the computer science registration line at Virginia Tech just five seconds before me in July 1971, taking the last spot in a class I needed, I probably would have spent the last twenty years in Houston as a chemical engineer. Instead, I had led an unbelievably adventurous life as a burn and transplant surgeon, and now as an Army officer. Even more incredibly, I was now involved in efforts to end the Cold War, and the Soviet Union considered me a hero. It all seemed like a dream.

The frigid wind and snow hitting my face was proof that it wasn't a dream. I took off my glove and stuck my hand into the railing on the side of the bridge, grabbed a handful of snow and tossed it over the side onto the frozen river below. *Yes*, I told myself as the cold snow stung my hand,

I am very much awake and this is all very real.

After about ten minutes of standing on the bridge, I walked back to the hotel. When I passed the two men at the end of the bridge, I nodded politely. One turned and followed me back to the hotel. The other remained at the edge of the bridge. I didn't give it a second's thought—just two men out walking around the city. I crawled into bed around midnight and promptly fell asleep.

The next morning, rested and mentally awake, I realized what I had done, and who had followed me. The scenario must have looked pretty suspicious to a couple of KGB agents. A U.S. Army major leaves his room in the middle of a blizzard at eleven o'clock at night to go stand on a bridge over the Moscow River. From a distance, they see him stick his hand into the railing on the side of the bridge and make a drop. One of the agents remains behind, waiting for a Soviet traitor to pick up the drop.

Of course, since no traitor showed up, the agent spent the rest of the night in a bitterly cold snowstorm. I kind of felt sorry for the guy. He was just doing his job, and I was making it awfully hard for him.

A Very Dry
Red Wine

IN MOSCOW, MY TWO COLLEAGUES AND I visited burn centers and took a tour of the Vishnevsky Institute of Surgery. The Institute was built as a center of scientific research during the Khrushchev era, and world-class researchers do some great work there. We spent a fun and informative day at the Institute, meeting with knowledgeable Soviet colleagues and learning about their surgery techniques, and they hosted a lunch for us.

The food was exotic by American standards: flaky smoked fish, caviar and hard-boiled eggs, borsht, grouse, veal tongue, pickled vegetables, and beef stroganoff loaded with cream. To wash it all down, we had unlimited bottles of sweet red wine (the water wasn't safe to drink, and vodka was traditionally saved for dinner).

One of the Soviet scientists sitting next to me watched me take a microsip of wine in between bites.

"How do you like our wines?" he asked.

I love a good dry red wine, but Russian red wine is so sweet it tastes like dessert. But since I was essentially on a diplomatic mission, I drank their red wines and pretended to like them.

"Oh, they're most memorable," I replied, smiling.

"Tell me," he said, laying down his fork. "What kind of wine do you drink in America?"

"Well, in Texas I tend to drink dry red wine," I responded. "We have some great wineries."

"What is 'dry wine'?" he asked, puzzled.

"It means a wine that isn't sweet," I explained. *Oops*, I thought. *Can I take that back?*

"Ahh," the scientist said, nodding.

He snapped his fingers in the air and a waiter suddenly appeared. The scientist said something to him in Russian, and the waiter bowed slightly and promptly hurried off to the kitchen.

"We too have dry red wines," the scientist said with a broad smile. "I have sent for a bottle for you to have with lunch. But in my country we don't refer to them as 'dry.' We call them 'naturally fermented.'"

I turned to the translator to make sure I had understood correctly.

"Naturally fermented?" I asked him, trying to hide my concern.

"Yes," he said. "That means the wine is fermented in a bottle without a cork."

I had a bachelor's degree in biochemistry, so I knew exactly what happens if you ferment a bottle of wine without a cork. As soon as the alcohol is formed, it continues to be metabolized through its combination with oxygen. This metabolic process continues until bacteria transforms all the alcohol into acetic acid—in layman's terms, vinegar.

Because I was a representative of the U.S. government, I would have to drink an entire bottle of vinegar with lunch to avoid creating a diplomatic incident. As the scientist had requested it just for me, it would be an unforgivable insult if I did not.

When the bottle arrived, the waiter filled my glass. Everyone at the table watched expectantly as I brought the glass under my nose and took a whiff. I couldn't even complete the inhalation process before I started to cough, and my host looked alarmed. To suppress my inadvertently rude cough, I quickly downed half the glass. My tongue recoiled inside my mouth, and my lips puckered. I fought off a reflexive gasp.

The Soviet scientist sitting next to me was eager for the verdict.

"How is it?" he asked. "It is not sweet, is it?"

"Oh no," I assured him, forcing a smile onto my severely puckered lips. "It is not at all sweet!"

"Not many Soviets like this type of wine," he admitted. "You Americans have a strong stomach!"

For the remainder of lunch, I would take as large a sip of the vinegar as I could, immediately fill my mouth with bread, cheese, meat, or whatever was available, then quickly swallow. It took every ounce of discipline I had to refrain from gagging. And I had to keep this up while carrying on pleasant conversation with our hosts.

I hope President Bush appreciates the sacrifice I'm making for my country and global diplomacy, I thought.

Toward the end of the meal, as that bottle from hell came closer and closer to being completely consumed, the Soviet scientist snapped his fingers and a waiter rushed over.

"Do you require a second bottle?" my host asked me.

"Oh, no no no," I assured him. "One bottle is quite sufficient. Thank you so much for your thoughtfulness."

Since that day, I have never, not once, put vinegar on my salad or dipped bread in it. If you think I'm overreacting, just try drinking a single glass of vinegar. Then imagine having to drink an entire bottle of the stuff. I think vodka tastes like rubbing alcohol or fingernail polish remover smells, but naturally fermented Russian wine makes vodka taste like dessert.

Ice Fishing
in Siberia

A FTER OUR TWO DAYS IN MOSCOW, we headed to Ufa on Aeroflot—yet another adventure. The Soviet airline was notorious around the world for catastrophic incidents; in the 1980s alone, Aeroflot planes were involved in fifteen deadly accidents that resulted in more than 2,000 deaths. I never took a safe flight for granted on that airline.

In Ufa, we gave lectures and attended meetings with experts on railway accidents, natural gas explosions, and burn care. We shared ideas and talked about what worked and what didn't when dealing with mass casualties and hundreds of survivors.

One day after giving a number of lectures, my colleagues and I were driven to a small spa about 150 miles outside Ufa. Like my trip to the banya, the drive to the spa was a scene out of *Doctor Zhivago*, with vast stretches of stark land covered with snow. Bill Becker, one of my colleagues, had come down with a bad cold but insisted on coming, so I gave him some advice on the drive.

"Just don't tell them you're sick," I warned him. "They'll try to make you better."

"I can't exactly hide it," Bill responded. "I'm blowing my nose every two minutes and look like hell. Besides, what's so bad about trying to make me better?"

"Don't say I didn't warn you," I said with a shrug.

When we arrived, our hosts greeted us with enthusiastic bear hugs and glasses of vodka. It only took a few seconds for the one in charge to notice Bill's bleary eyes and flushed face, and the Russian gripped him firmly by the shoulders.

"You are not so well!" Sergei exclaimed, concerned.

The rest of the men nodded their heads and looked worried. A few of them started talking in Russian, gesturing at my friend.

Sergei clapped his hands loudly, silencing the hubbub.

"We have best therapy for you!" he said. "Come!"

He escorted Bill to a private room in the spa, where two assistants stripped him of all his clothes and slathered his entire body with a thick layer of honey. They wrapped him up in a sheet like a mummy and laid him down on a cot in the corner. Bill mumbled something and struggled to get up.

"You must rest quietly!" one of the spa assistants scolded, wagging her finger at him.

Since Bill couldn't really move, he had no choice but to obey.

Meanwhile, our hosts were presenting my other colleague and me with two options for our afternoon's entertainment.

"We go bear hunting, or we go ice fishing!" Sergei said enthusiastically. "These are two favorite Russian activities! You choose!"

My colleague and I quickly weighed the two choices and considered the relative danger. After a fifteen-second discussion, we chose ice fishing.

We took a brief hike to a frozen lake, and I looked around expectantly, searching for the fishing poles and ice saws. I didn't see any. Our friends had already pulled out their bottles of vodka and were laughing rowdily, and I quickly clued in. Aha! They had no interest in sitting in the middle of a frozen lake. "Ice fishing" was merely an excuse for their actual favorite pastime: drinking vodka and telling stories. That was just fine with us.

Eventually, though, my fingers started going numb and I couldn't move my tongue very well. Pretending to catch fish in sub-zero weather seemed a little pointless.

"You know, I bet the vodka tastes just as good inside the warm *dacha*," I suggested.

Our hosts looked stunned, as though they'd never thought of that. We made a hasty retreat into the spa, where we continued drinking and laughing until very late. Meanwhile, my poor sick friend was lying on a cot with a honey-coated sheet wrapped tightly around him.

I woke up in the morning with a terrible hangover—only the second one I'd ever had. Bill, however, had a larger problem: the honey had hardened, effectively gluing the sheet to his skin. When Sergei checked in on him in the morning, Bill graciously thanked him for the wonderful "cure" and asked where the shower was.

"Shower?" Sergei responded. "So sorry, we have no shower."

"Oh, okay," Bill said, scratching at the sheet. "Could you direct me to a bathtub?"

"No, no, we have no bathtub here!" Sergei said, laughing. *Those silly Americans!*

It turned out there was no running water at this spa. The only water was the bottled kind we'd brought with us.

Bill improvised a plan. He slowly shuffled into the sauna, and stayed until he was sweating enough to loosen the sheet from his body. Of course, this didn't remove the honey. At this point, he had two choices: he could ride back to Ufa stark naked, or he could put clothes on over his honey-coated body. He opted for clothes, and sat very uncomfortably during the three-hour ride back to Ufa.

After a very long, lukewarm shower, Bill was able to peel off his clothes and thoroughly scrub off the honey. He was relieved to be clean, but no, his cold wasn't any better.

Welcome
to Russia

IN DECEMBER 1991, I returned to Ufa for the last time. By this time I was on the faculty at the University of Texas Medical Branch, and no longer on active duty. I brought three colleagues with me, two of whom had never been to the Soviet Union. As it turned out, they still can't say they've ever been there.

Sometime between takeoff in Dallas, Texas, and landing in Frankfurt, Germany, the Soviet Union ceased to exist. Boris Yeltsin announced that the Union of Soviet Socialist Republics had been dissolved and each of the former republics was now an independent country. He also banned communist activities, and worldwide Stalinism collapsed. All of that happened while we were 30,000 feet in the air.

When we arrived in Frankfurt to change planes to Moscow, we sat down at an airport bar and ordered some well-deserved drinks. CNN News came on TV with the breaking story, and the entire place fell silent. Of all the times to fly to the Soviet Union, I thought, I would have to pick the day when the Soviet Union no longer existed. Somewhat concerned, I wondered whether the military would stage a violent coup in a last-ditch effort to save the country. What about the KGB? After all, the hard-liners of the Communist Party had attempted a coup against Gorbachev just a few months earlier. Would we land to find ourselves in the middle of a civil war?

For the three-hour flight from Frankfurt to Moscow, I was seated in business class, right behind the cockpit. Adding to my concerns about the dissolution of the country, the pilot began leaving the cockpit every twenty minutes or so to go to the lavatory. After about his fourth trip, I intercepted him when he got out.

"Excuse me, Captain," I said quietly, introducing myself. "I'm a doctor. Are you sick? I'm sure I have a medication that could help."

He peaked over my shoulder and moved us closer to the cockpit.

"Yeah, I'm sick all right," he whispered, "but it's nothing you can fix."

I raised my eyebrows in concern.

"I've got a bit of a problem," he said.

Suddenly I started to feel sick myself. No one wants to hear their pilot say those words.

"There's no more Soviet Union," he said, grimacing.

I nodded, finally exhaling. *Oh that*, I thought, relieved.

"Yes, amazing, isn't it?" I responded. "I never thought it would happen in my lifetime."

"Well, yes it is, but my problem is I can't raise Moscow's air-traffic controller," he said, visibly worried.

What the hell?

"And you've tried going, "Moscow, Moscow, come in, please" into the radio?" I asked.

"Yup," he responded. "Been doing that for the past two hours. Nothing but static."

"Hmm," I said. "If there's a coup, the first thing leaders would do is shut down all communications."

The pilot nodded.

I began to think that I might need the lavatory as much as the pilot did.

"Hey, I speak a little Russian," I said helpfully. "In case you hear anything."

"Thanks," he said, clapping me on the arm. "I'll come get you if I do."

He returned to the cockpit. Fifteen minutes later, he came back out again and went into the lavatory. I was waiting for him when he came out, and offered what I thought was an excellent suggestion.

"Why don't you turn the plane around and head back to Germany?" I proposed.

He shook his head firmly.

"Very bad idea," he said. "We've been warned for years that if we deviated from our assigned route over the Soviet Union, they'd shoot us down."

For a second I thought he was kidding. Then I remembered the Korean Airliner that had deviated a few miles off course about ten years before, and had promptly been shot down by the Soviet Air Force. I decided to not offer any more suggestions.

Eventually the pilot landed the Delta jet on the runway at Sheremetyevo International Airport, without ever hearing a peep from the tower until just prior to touchdown. Instead of pulling up to the terminal, the pilot slowly took the aircraft to the end of the taxiway adjacent to the runway, then put it in park. He came out a minute later and made a beeline for the lavatory.

"So what's going on?" I whispered, grabbing him by the elbow as he came out. "Why are we out here? What'd they say? Are they going to let us in?"

The pilot shrugged.

"They told me to just park here," he said. "I'm not asking any questions, and I'm not going out until they tell me to."

I nodded in agreement.

"Are you going to make an announcement?"

He shook his head.

"I'll wait until I know more. I don't want the passengers to get nervous."

As one of the passengers, I can assure you we were already damn nervous.

We sat on the edge on the runway for thirty-five minutes. We peered out the little windows anxiously, scanning the darkened airport for signs of tanks and armored personnel carriers. As an experienced traveler to Moscow, I tried to assure my fellow passengers that there was nothing to worry about, just a normal routine trip to the Soviet Union—er, Russia—or whatever the hell they were calling the country at this particular minute. I assumed it was still a country.

Finally a bus pulled up to the plane and we were ordered to get on. I hung back, waiting for everyone else to get off first. (I had learned my lesson in China.)

The pilot finally motioned me to go.

"You first," he said.

"Is it too late to go back to Germany?" I asked.

"We don't have enough fuel," he said, shrugging. Clearly, he had considered it.

The bus took us to the terminal, and we filed up to go through customs. As the tallest in the crowd, I had the advantage of a clear view over everyone's heads, and I didn't see any military police. I began to breathe normally. When it was my turn, I walked up to the customs window and held out my passport.

The customs agent looked at it, then looked at me.

"What is the purpose of your visit?" she said, stone-faced.

"Business," I said. "I'm a surgeon."

She stamped the passport and handed it back to me.

"Welcome to Russia, Mr. Waymack," she said with a hint of a smile. "I hope you enjoy your stay here."

"Thank you!" I responded, "I'm sure I will."

It's not just that I was relieved I hadn't been sent to a gulag and no KGB agents were tailing me. I was happy and optimistic because I was in a beautiful country with friends I had grown to love, and communism had fallen. It was a wonderful way to end my time as a surgeon in Siberia.

Epilogue

I N THE FALL OF 1996, five years after my last trip to Ufa, my career
as a trauma surgeon was coming to an end. I was on the faculty of the
University of Medicine and Dentistry of New Jersey, where I was both
a surgeon and director of the Surgical Intensive Care Unit. I had accepted
a position with a pharmaceutical development consulting firm in Washington, D.C., and would be leaving in just a few weeks.

In my capacity as director, I made rounds every morning with the surgery residents on all the patients in the ICU. During rounds, the residents
would present the current status of all the patients as well as their plans for
the treatment of the patients. I would listen and offer suggestions.

One morning shortly before I left New Jersey, the residents began to present
the patients to me. Everything seemed to be routine and straightforward until
we reached the room of a new patient who had been admitted the night
before. He had been found lying in the street in a coma, apparently due to
an assault. One thing I knew for sure was that the patient had Asian ancestry.

The resident began his presentation.

"This is Li Roi Wun," he said. "He was admitted last night after being
assaulted. Among other injuries, he suffered severe intracranial injuries, a
broken arm, and two broken ribs. His Glasgow coma scale is a six."

"What does the CT scan show?" I asked the resident.

"Li Roi's CT showed edema but no intracranial bleeding," he answered.

"Has neurosurgery seen Mr. Wun this morning?"

"Not yet, but they should be by to see Li Roi soon."

The resident kept referring to the patient by his first and middle names,
which I found disrespectful. Then it occurred to me that I might be the
guilty party—after all, in Asia, people frequently give their surnames first.

"Is his first name Li or Wun?" I asked.

The entire team looked confused.

"Dr. Waymack, he's Li Roi Wun," the resident said.

"Oh. So his given name is Li Roi?"

They still looked confused.

"Yes, Li Roi," the resident said slowly, showing me the patient's chart. "Li Roi Wun."

At the top of the chart I saw "Leroy 1" written where the patient's name should go.

"Huh?!"

"Dr. Waymack, didn't you get the memo?" the resident asked.

What memo? I thought. I get dozens every day and don't have time to read them all.

"Maybe not. What did it say?"

"It said the hospital is replacing its method of identifying John Does," the resident explained.

For decades, the hospital had been temporarily naming unconscious, unidentifiable patients according to their race, gender, and sequence for that year. Thus, the first unidentifiable white female patient admitted to the hospital each year would be named Unknown White Female One. The second such patient would be Unknown White Female Two. The first unknown black male patient would be named Unknown Black Male One, and so on.

The resident continued describing the contents of the memo.

"Someone apparently complained that this was a prejudicial naming system since there were always far more unknown black males than unknown black females, or unknown white males, or unknown white females."

"But why is that prejudicial?" I asked.

"Well, because 'Unknown Black Male 45' makes it seem as if black males are more likely to arrive at the hospital in a comatose state than women or whites."

I wasn't sympathetic. Or politically correct.

"Yeah, that's what big numbers tend to do," I said. "They seem to always imply they are larger than smaller numbers."

I took a deep breath.

"Let me see if I have this correct," I continued. "This patient arrives in the ER last night, comatose, no identification."

"Correct."

"So the computer then gives him the name of Leroy."

"Correct. And since he is the first Leroy of this year, he is Leroy One."

I thought back to my days as a third-year student in the labor and delivery suites, having to deal with the babies' often unpronounceable and un-spellable names. I thought back to all the other moments of confusion that had occurred during the past twenty years. Somehow, it seemed a fitting finale to my career as a surgeon.

"Fine," I said. "Let me know what the neurosurgeons have to say about Mr. One's condition."

A few weeks later, I left the often-insane world of trauma surgery to become a consultant in the field of pharmaceutical development. It had been an extraordinary two decades as a trauma surgeon, researcher, and professor. Though I looked forward to the challenges of my new duties as a consultant, I was sure I would never experience the kinds of bizarre incidents I've recorded here.

On the other hand, even pharmaceutical companies must have their versions of Crazy Betty and naked patients. I'll record their anecdotes if they do.

ABOUT THE AUTHOR

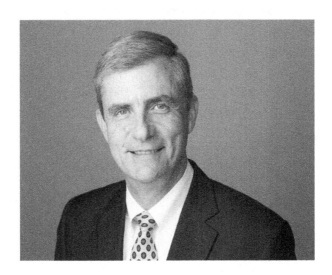

J. Paul Waymack, M.D., Sc.D., is the founder, chairman, and chief medical officer of Kitov Pharmaceuticals, a drug development company. He received a bachelor's degree from Virginia Tech, a Doctor of Medicine degree from the Medical College of Virginia, and a Doctor of Science degree from the University of Cincinnati. An experienced clinical surgeon, Dr. Waymack was an associate professor of surgery at the University of Texas Medical Branch and the University of Medicine and Dentistry of New Jersey. He has published more than one hundred scientific essays, mainly in the fields of prostaglandins and immunology.

Dr. Waymack was commissioned a major in the U.S. Army Medical Corps, where he served as surgeon and chief of surgical studies at the Army Burn Center, operated by the U.S. Army Institute of Surgical Research. During the height of the Cold War, President George H.W. Bush sent Dr. Waymack to the Soviet Union to assist in the emergency treatment of hundreds of burn victims after a disastrous train accident.

He has more than twenty years of experience in the biopharma field as a drug-development consultant for major pharmaceutical companies, including Pfizer, Roche, Pharmacia, Warner Lambert, and Searle, and served as medical reviewer and special consultant to the U.S. Food and Drug Administration Center for Drug Evaluation and Research. Before founding Kitov Pharmaceuticals, Dr. Waymack had an international clientele of pharmaceutical companies in the United States, the Far East, the Middle East, and Europe.

Dr. Waymack lives in Washington, D.C., with his wife, Barbara, and their two sons.

ABOUT THE EDITOR

Elayne Wells Harmer is a writer, editor, and attorney. In 1987, she graduated from Stanford University with a B.A. in English. After working as a journalist in both broadcast and print media, she received a J.D. from the University of Utah College of Law. She was an attorney for the Salt Lake City law firm Fabian & Clendenin, specializing in employment litigation, and served as legislative counsel to Senator Slade Gorton (R-WA) in Washington, D.C., advising him on issues arising before the U.S. Senate Labor Committee.

For seven years, Elayne was managing editor at RMS Productions in Salt Lake City, where she co-wrote and edited numerous books on military history. Currently a freelance writer and editor, she edits books covering a wide range of topics. Her books cover a wide range of topics, including business, adventure, religion, psychology, military history, corporate history, and memoirs.

Elayne was born in Argentina and spent much of her youth in various Latin American countries. She and her husband, David, have four children and live in Utah.

Made in the USA
Monee, IL
13 December 2020